COUNTRY
ENTERTAINING

COUNTRY
ENTERTAINING

BONNIE TANDY LEBLANG

COURAGE
BOOKS

An Imprint of Running Press Book Publishers
Philadelphia, Pennsylvania

© Jeff McNamara

COUNTRY ENTERTAINING
was prepared and produced by
Michael Friedman Publishing Group, Inc.
15 West 26th Street
New York, New York 10010

Editor: Elizabeth Viscott Sullivan
Art Director: Jeff Batzli
Designer: Kevin Ullrich
Photography Editor: Daniella Jo Nilva

Typeset by The Interface Group, Inc.
Color separations by Excel Graphic Arts Ltd.
Printed in Hong Kong by Leefung-Asco Printers Ltd.

This book may be ordered from the Publisher.
Please include $2.50 for postage and handling for each copy.
But try your bookstore first!

Published by Courage Books
An imprint of Running Press
125 South Twenty-second Street
Philadelphia, Pennsylvania 19103

Acknowledgments

Thanks to Joanne—whose passion is country—for half the work.

Thanks to the Alaska Seafood Marketing Institute, American Lamb Council, California Strawberry Advisory Board, California Tree Fruit Agreement, Franklin Mushroom Farms, Inc., George Dickel, German Wine Information Bureau, Hershey Foods Corporation, Jarlsberg Norwegian Cheese, Kahlúa Kitchens, Libby's Division of Carnation Company, Rudolf Müller GMBH & Co., National Broiler Council, National Goose Council, National Pork Producers Council, National Turkey Federation, Norseland Foods, Reynolds Wrap Kitchens, Saco Foods, P.J. Valckenberg, W. Atlee Burpee and Company, and the Wisconsin Milk Marketing Board for their contributions.

C O N T

INTRODUCTION 10

WINTER 12

Woodstove Supper 16
Sleigh Bells
    and Hay Baskets 20
Christmas in the Country 24
Hearthside Picnic 30
Country Valentine Supper 36
Sugaring Party 40

SPRING 44

Seed Catalog Time 48
Fleeting Tastes of Spring 52
Derby Day Buffet 56
Strawberry Festival 60
Spring Showers Picnic 64
German Wine Festival 68

SUMMER 74

Old-Fashioned Clambake 78
Country Fair Sampler 84
Cornhusking Supper 88
Too Many Zucchini 92
Herb and Flower Garden
    Luncheon 96
Ranch Barbecue 102

E N T S

AUTUMN 108

Harvest Festival 112
Pumpkin Time Dinner 116
New England
  Thanksgiving 120
Rag Dolls and
  Sugar Cookies 126
Lunch Basket Traditions 130
Country Breakfast 134

**COOKWARE AND
BAKEWARE
EQUIVALENTS** 138

**WEIGHT AND
VOLUME EQUIVALENTS
(VEGETABLES)** 139

**WEIGHT AND
VOLUME EQUIVALENTS
(FRUITS)** 140

KITCHEN METRICS 141

Introduction

Country is a state of mind. Whether you live in an eighteenth-century farmhouse or a city apartment, surrounding yourself with the simple trappings of times past gives a sense of serenity in the comfort of familiar surroundings—an escape from the stress and insecurity of today's fast-paced world.

Country style is the result of old-world traditions adapted to a new climate and blended with the native products of a new land. The waves of settlers who came to North America to start a new life brought with them a treasury of customs and foodways from their homelands. In order to survive in their adopted home, they had to rapidly incorporate the new native abundance into their original customs. The homes and household furnishings that evolved from this meshing of cultures provided comfort and security amidst the hardships of colonial life; the foodways that emerged ensured survival. In fact, the interaction of these many cultures produced the tapestry of regional specialties and customs we see in North America today. These special tastes and surroundings that meant the good life in early times still offer the same sense of comfort and security.

Sharing has always been a country tradition. Work shared goes twice as quickly; food shared tastes twice as good. Old-time country occasions were always planned around food, whether to celebrate survival through a time of hardship, banish sadness in times of grief, reward a job well done, mark the occasions of life, or strengthen the bonds of love and friendship. *Country Entertaining* reflects the graciousness of yesterday's welcome, provides the taste memories of some of our favorite foods, and enables readers to share the joy of our country heritage with those who are special enough to entertain at home.

Country life is close to nature, and takes its cues from the seasons. In the spring, the awakening meadows provide us with tender young greens and baskets of berries. In the summer, orchards, fields, and gardens abound with fresh fruit and vegetables—bushels of colorful peppers, sweet corn, and tomatoes—still warm from the summer sun. Autumn harvests nuts, apples, and roots to be carefully stored away for later feasts. Winter brings folks in from the cold to enjoy the bounty stored away in the three previous seasons, and to dream of the first dish of fresh strawberries as spring starts the cycle all over again. *Country Entertaining* helps us to share the bounty of North America's fields and forests, enjoy the occasions of the year, great or small, and create an atmosphere of warmth in which family and guests will feel cared for.

Wherever you live, enjoying country fare in season gives you a sense of order in life. In a time of world marketing seasons, hypermarkets, and packaging that extends shelf life for weeks, fresh foods from the garden or farm root you in the flow of nature's seasons—in the traditions of our past. *Country Entertaining* is a life-style guide to help you plan special occasions throughout the year. Foods and entertainments are merely suggestions to get you started. If items suggested are not available in your area, substitute a local specialty. Country is a style that can bring the warmth of old-fashioned hospitality to your party, no matter where it is to be held.

WINTER

Woodstove Supper

Sleigh Bells and Hay Baskets

Christmas in the Country

Hearthside Picnic

Country Valentine Supper

Sugaring Party

Winter is the perfect time for fireside entertaining. Whether in a stove or fireplace, a roaring fire should be the focal point of your country welcome. Cook hearty dishes, such as chili, on your woodstove or heat quick-cooking but slow-serving dishes, such as Raclette, at hearthside. Either way, you'll warm your guest's bodies as well as their souls.

Be sure your guests are dressed appropriately for the cold weather, so you can move part or all of your gathering outside to enjoy the crisp, clean winter air. Pack a selection of robust foods into a hay-lined basket and plan a hayride to a local pond where you can have a picnic before or after ice skating.

Special foods, such as maple syrup, should be enjoyed in their season. Plan a party around this special food, or, if your area doesn't produce fresh maple syrup, choose a local specialty to celebrate. In winter, any reason to frolic is worthwhile.

In most places, winter brings holiday celebrations indoors, whether for a large family Christmas gathering or a Valentine's Day party for two. To make these occasions truly festive, it is important to pay as much attention to decorating your house and table as to the food you serve. Of course, at all occasions, nothing is more important than your guests.

Woodstove Supper

Menu:

❧❧❧

Beef and Chicken Chili with Assorted Toppings

Country Corn Bread

Avocado Salad

Bartlett Pear Squares with Whipped Cream or Ice Cream

Beer or Chilled Cider

When Count Rumford developed the woodstove shortly after America's Revolutionary War, he caused a revolution in the kitchen. Country cooks who had been scorching their eyebrows bending over an open fireplace were delighted. Once a more reliable oven was available, home bakers immediately started turning out treats as never before. The fragrant aroma of breads, pies, puddings, cookies, and cobblers filled kitchens everywhere, and dessert became an important part of family meals. The woodstove not only made meals easier to prepare, it frequently provided the warmest, most comfortable spot in the home. Gradually, the woodstove replaced the hearth as the center of family life. And today, on a cold winter evening, there is still no more friendly and welcoming spot for informal entertaining than around a well-polished, cast-iron woodstove.

The Woodstove Supper is a kitchen party. Since the kitchen is usually reserved for family and very special friends, most guests feel quite privileged to be entertained there. Your tabletop and service need not be fancy, as the informality of the kitchen lends itself to the simplicity of a well-used wooden table set with pottery, sturdy tumblers, and homespun napkins. A centerpiece of dried flowers in a gathering basket or seasonal fruit in a hand-hewn wooden bowl sets the mood. The woodstove is an excellent warming surface; the chili and corn bread will stay at the perfect temperature all through

This Rugby, Tennessee, woodstove produces hearty country fare and invites family gatherings.

Corn chips and shredded cheese top a steaming bowl of beef and chicken chili.

Count Rumford was quite a colorful character. Born in New England in 1753 as Benjamim Thompson, he made a living as a scientist and inventor. When the Revolutionary War started, he was suddenly banished from the colonies (for spying, it is rumored). He moved to England and then to Bavaria, where he was made Count Rumford for his service to Karl Theodor, the ruler of Bavaria. In addition to the woodstove, he is credited with the invention of the double boiler, tea kettle, and drip coffee pot.

🌰 🌰 🌰

A well-seasoned cast-iron skillet insures perfectly baked corn bread with a crispy crust.

the meal when kept on it. The salad and toppings should be served from a nearby sideboard or table.

Plan a menu of the food that a woodstove cooks best—food that requires long baking or slow simmering. Corn bread and Bartlett pear squares can be made several hours ahead, then rewarmed in the pans they were baked in originally, and served from the top of the woodstove. About 1½ hours before serving time, start the chili in a large, heavy stewpot or Dutch oven. Add quartered, boneless chicken thighs and chunks of lean beef to your favorite chili recipe in place of the meat you usually use. Let the chili simmer on the top of the woodstove to gather flavor until you are ready to serve it.

Prepare the salad of mixed greens ahead of time; cover with a linen towel and refrigerate. At the last minute, slice an avocado and toss the slices with lemon juice, then add them to the salad along with a coriander dressing. While the chili is simmering, you can set up a lazy Susan of toppings, such as shredded Cheddar, Monterey Jack, or Jalapeño cheese, chopped red or green sweet peppers, corn chips, chopped green onions, and/or coriander leaves. Guests can select their favorite toppings to add to either the chili or the salad. When all is ready, tie a checked linen towel to the handle of the lid for a pot holder, and let guests serve themselves right from the pot. Leave plenty of time for second helpings. Clear the table while your guests serve themselves warm Bartlett pear squares from the woodstove; top the squares with whipped cream or ice cream.

Bartlett Pear Squares

Makes 8 servings

Filling:

3 or 4   fresh Bartlett pears
¼   cup cornstarch
⅓   cup sugar
¼   teaspoon salt
½   teaspoon ground cinnamon
¾   cup water
2½   tablespoons freshly squeezed lemon juice
2   tablespoons (¼ stick) unsalted butter
1   teaspoon vanilla extract
2   tablespoons currants or raisins

Pastry shell and topping:

2   cups unbleached all-purpose flour
½   teaspoon salt
5   tablespoons sugar
12   tablespoons (1½ sticks) unsalted butter, softened
3   egg yolks
1½   tablespoons freshly squeezed lemon juice
¼   cup ground walnuts

For the filling, pare, halve, core, and slice the pears to measure 4 cups. Toss with 2 tablespoons cornstarch. In a saucepan, combine the sugar, the remaining cornstarch, salt, and cinnamon. Stir in the water and lemon juice, and cook, stirring, over medium heat until thickened. Add the butter and vanilla; stir in the pears and currants.

For the pastry shell and topping, mix the flour, salt, and 3 tablespoons of the sugar in a bowl; cut in the butter with a pastry blender until well blended, moist, and crumbly. Mix in the egg yolks and lemon juice. Save 1 cup of dough for the topping; press the remainder into the bottom and 1¼ inches up the sides of an 8-inch square baking pan. Bake in a 375°F oven for 10 minutes. Pour in the pear filling.

For the crumbly topping, add the remaining 2 tablespoons sugar and the walnuts to the reserved 1 cup dough; crumble over the filling. Bake 35 to 40 minutes longer.

Cut into squares. Serve either warm or chilled.

Recipe courtesy of the California Tree Fruit Agreement

© Anita Sabarese

Ripe and succulent California pears await harvest and storage for midwinter enjoyment.

Sleigh Bells and Hay Baskets

Menu:

❧❧❧

Beef and Mushroom Stew

Hot Buttered Biscuits

Warm Rum-Spiked Rice Pudding

Hot Buttered Rum, Hot Chocolate, and Coffee

Long before ice chests were invented, people had an ingenious way of keeping hot food and cold food at appropriate temperatures. They filled an apple crate or bushel basket with hay, wrapped the hot or cold dishes in several layers of quilts, and then nestled the quilt-wrapped food into the hay.

Just after the first snow, once a nearby pond or lake has frozen over, invite some friends for a brisk sleigh ride through the woods to an ice-skating party. Tell your friends to dress warmly, to dig through their drawers for their thermal underwear, and to bring their ice skates. The entire evening's festivities will be held outdoors.

In preparation for a Sleigh Bells and Hay Baskets party, assemble your old fruit baskets and crates, or take a trip to a local farm or orchard to purchase them for packing the food. In addition to the wooden crates, you'll need lots of hay—both to line the crates or baskets and, of course, to fill the sleigh. Have a huge pile of woolen blankets for the sleigh ride. Be sure to have enough blankets on hand so that everyone can

be wrapped snugly, and bring along extra scarves and gloves in case someone has forgotten his or hers.

Into a burlap sack, pack a lot of kindling and enough logs of dry wood to keep a fire going all evening, then store the sack at the front of the sleigh. Adorn the sides of the sleigh with strips of sleigh bells to jingle in time with the horses as they trot through the snow-covered meadow. Fill a crate or basket with silverware, napkins, and earthenware bowls for the stew and rice pudding, as well as mugs for the beverages. Tuck in a box of wooden matches for lighting the fire, and bring along some marshmallows to toast. You might want to pack a flashlight just in case there's an emergency.

For this cold winter's night of skating on the pond, serve hot, hearty food in a bowl or a mug. In addition to warming your innards, the bowls or mugs can serve as hand warmers. Make an easy-to-prepare stew that sits on the stove or in the oven unattended, while you're readying the sleigh. Try a beef and mushroom stew in which almost all the ingredients are tossed

Nothing says country like a horse-drawn sleigh ride through a snow-covered meadow.

into a pot or Dutch oven and simmered for hours. This is one stew where there's no need to brown the meat, so it's perfect to take traveling as well as to enjoy inside by a roaring fire.

Line with hay the empty wooden crates or bushel baskets that you've collected. Be sure the lid of the Dutch oven in which you've cooked the stew fits tightly. If not, tightly wrap the Dutch oven in foil first. Wrap the casserole with bath towels, then enclose it in a heavy quilt along with some freshly baked buttered biscuits. Be sure to wrap the biscuits in a linen napkin and then in a bath towel before you put them in the quilt with the casserole. Nestle the quilt-wrapped casserole and biscuits into the hay-lined basket, and store it on the sleigh.

Try to time the rum-spiked pudding to come out of the oven just before guests arrive. Wrap it in a towel, then in a blanket or quilt, put it into another hay basket, and store it on the sleigh.

If you can't locate wooden crates or baskets, just wrap the casseroles in foil, towels, and a heavy blanket, and firmly nestle them into the hay under the wooden benches on the sleigh.

On a chilly winter night, guests will drink many hot beverages to try to keep themselves warm, so bring more drinks than you think you may need. While preparing the beverages, such as hot chocolate, hot buttered rum, and coffee, fill the thermoses with boiling water. This will warm the containers and allow them to better retain heat, which will keep the beverages piping hot. Once the containers are warmed, pour out the water, and fill them with the drinks you've prepared. Then you can store them on the sleigh in a basket with the mugs.

Once your friends arrive, check to see if they're dressed warmly, and offer scarves and gloves to those who may have forgotten them. Hand out heavy blankets, and direct everyone onto the sleigh. Some lucky folks will sit in the hay next to the warm hay baskets filled with the night's supper. Then let the sleigh festivities begin!

The driver directs the horse-driven sleigh around the barn, along the trickling, still unfrozen stream and through the hilly meadow toward the pond. As the moon glistens on the fresh fallen snow why not start the evening off with a chorus of "Jingle Bells?" Singing will create a magical mood, and once the singing starts, it won't be difficult to keep the melodies flowing until the sleigh pulls to a halt near the pond.

As soon as you arrive, have someone pour hot buttered rum for the adults, and hot cocoa for the children. Everyone can enjoy the clear, star-filled evening as you start a bonfire. Ask one person to clear away the snow in a small area, and another to bring the wood-filled burlap bag and matches from the sleigh to the clearing. Start the fire and let the fun really begin!

After a few games of tag on the ice, everyone will appreciate a steaming bowl of stew. You'll be amazed at how

The aroma of freshly baked biscuits still warm from the oven heightens folks' appetites.

quickly the stew and biscuits disappear. A cold night of outdoor games certainly heightens anyone's appetite.

Send everyone back to the ice for another game after the meal. Try a game of freeze tag—if you're tagged by the person who's "it," you must stand still until freed by another player. Once this game is complete, your guests will be ready for some warm rice pudding and coffee or more hot chocolate.

At the end of the evening, just before heading back home on the sleigh, gather everyone around the warm fire. While your friends are removing their skates, pass out some of the sticks that were packed for kindling and—as a nostalgic treat—hand out some marshmallows to toast.

As everyone snuggles into the sleigh for the ride home, start the singing again.

BAKED BEEF AND MUSHROOM STEW

Makes 6 to 8 servings

2　pounds lean beef, cut into 1¼-inch cubes
4　large carrots, cut into 1-inch slices
3　stalks celery, cut into 1-inch slices
2　medium onions, cut into eighths
1　large clove garlic, minced
2　1-pound cans whole peeled tomatoes
2　bay leaves
Freshly ground black pepper
½　teaspoon salt (optional)
1　10-ounce package frozen peas, thawed
1½　pounds mushrooms, cleaned

Preheat the oven to 300°F.

Place the beef, carrots, celery, onions, garlic, tomatoes, bay leaves, salt, and pepper to taste into a 3-quart Dutch oven. Cover and bake for 3½ hours or until the beef cubes are tender. Add the peas and mushrooms and bake an additional 15 minutes. Remove and discard the bay leaves.

Recipe courtesy of Franklin Mushroom Farms, Inc., North Franklin, Connecticut

Served in a copper pot, this beef and mushroom stew is elegant, but oh-so-easy.

Christmas in the Country

Menu:

🌰 🌰 🌰

Seafood Chowder

Roast Goose with Muscadine Sauce

Chestnut Stuffing

Candied Sweet Potatoes with Apples

Succotash

Cranberry Salad

Parker House Rolls

Mince or Apple Pie with Cinnamon Ice Cream

Coffee or Herb Teas

In colonial times, Christmas was not a major holiday. Midwinter celebrations were more likely to center around New Year's Day. Not until the late nineteenth century did Christmas feasting take on the emphasis it commands today.

Christmas falls at an opportune time of the year—the autumn harvest has just been stored away, hunting season is at its peak, and the last remaining vegetables of summer, carefully stored in the root cellar, are awaiting the midwinter feast. Just at the moment when the bleakness of winter sets in with great seriousness, when winter solstice brings the longest night of the year, Christmas provides the joy of giving and gathering with loved ones, and the occasion for the best and biggest of

© Jeff Greenberg

A Christmas day snow dusts the evergreens on this Swanzy, New Hampshire, farm.

Christmas is a time to enjoy the company of loved ones.

entertainments—Christmas dinner. The memory of this wonderful feast sustains food-lovers until the first dandelion and rhubarb of spring.

The preparations for Christmas dinner should be savored and enjoyed for weeks in advance. About a month before, fruitcakes should be made, so they can rest and gradually take in the moisture and flavor of a bourbon bath. Traditional European holiday cookies, such as Lebkuchen, Pfeffernuesse, and Springerle, should be made next, then stored away to mellow and soften into toothsome perfection.

A week or so before the celebration, decorate the house with fragrant greens, pine cones, and ribbons. Prepare additional cookie doughs, such as shortbread, sugar, gingerbread, and chocolate chip. If desired, bake the cookies and store them in a holiday tin in a cool, dry place. Or, if the next week's schedule is not too hectic, freeze the doughs and bake the cookies just a few days before Christmas. Chances of there being some left for Santa are much greater that way!

At least a day before the celebration, tuck small red apples and green pears into the arrangements of greens around the house. Add leaves to your dining table to accommodate the crowd you are expecting, or set up enough small tables for all the guests. Christmas is an occasion to use your special linens, so if you don't have family heirlooms, why not buy something special and start a family tradition? Red, green, or white are the colors of choice; napkins can match or coordinate with the tablecloth. For an interesting setting, alternate red, green, and white napkins around the table. (Buy enough of each color so that you will be able to use them for smaller crowds and other occasions; for example, you can use the red for Valentine's Day, the green for St. Patrick's Day.) Decorate the center of the table with an arrangement of greens, fruits, and colorful ribbons; tuck a few assorted nuts, still in their shells, into the greens. Arrange an assortment of holiday candles around the house, but be careful not to set them too close to flammable greens.

The day before Christmas, make sure you have everything on hand that you are going to need, such as milk for the children, cream for the coffee, and butter for the rolls. Make the base for the seafood chowder by preparing your favorite potato chowder recipe. The chestnut stuffing, jellied cranberry salad, rolls, and pies can all be completed ahead of time; wrap these items tightly, and refrigerate everything but the rolls. After you clean up the kitchen, put on some holiday music and relax to enjoy Christmas Eve with your family and friends.

Early Christmas morning (or at least 5 hours before dinner is to be served), stuff the goose and put it in the oven to roast according to the directions that follow. (Never stuff a bird ahead of time; stuffing can be an excellent medium for the growth of bacteria from poultry drippings.) Set the pies out in a spot where they won't be in the way, to allow them to warm to room temperature.

About 45 minutes before serving, prepare the candied sweet potatoes and

The aroma of cookies baking heralds the arrival of the holiday season.

© Steven Mark Needham/Envision

Offer guests a warm cup of seafood chowder as they come in from the cold.

There never was such a goose. Bob said he didn't believe there ever was such a goose cooked. Its tenderness and flavor, size and cheapness were the themes of universal admiration. Eked out by apple-sauce and mashed potatoes, it was sufficient dinner for the whole family; indeed, as Mrs. Cratchit said with great delight (surveying one small atom of a bone upon the dish) they hadn't at it all at last! Yet every one had had enough, and the youngest Cratchits in particular were steeped in sage and onion to the eyebrows.

 Charles Dickens,
A Christmas Carol

The holiday goose at the center of a spread of classic accompaniments.

apples, succotash, and a muscadine sauce from the goose broth and muscadine jelly. Warm the soup; add a variety of seafood, and cook it just until the seafood is cooked through. To make the cinnamon ice cream, allow vanilla ice cream to soften slightly, then swirl cinnamon through it; place it in the refrigerator (not freezer) during dinner and serve it slightly soft.

When all is ready, garnish the goose with grapes and sage leaves. Light your Christmas candles and let the joyous feast begin.

> *What is sauce for the goose may be sauce for the gander, but it is not necessarily sauce for the chicken, the duck, the turkey or the Guinea hen.*
>
> *Alice B. Toklas*

ROAST GOOSE

Thaw according to following directions. Preheat oven to 400°F. Remove neck and giblets from body cavity and use for stuffing, or refrigerate until ready to use. Remove excess fat from body cavity and neck skin. Rinse bird and drain.

To stuff, fill neck and body cavity loosely. Fasten neck skin to back, and tie legs together. Place goose, breast side up, on rack in shallow pan. Prick goose well. Insert thermometer deep into inside thigh muscle. Roast uncovered for 45 minutes to 1 hour (see chart) in preheated 400°F oven. During roasting, spoon or siphon off accumulated fat every 30 minutes. Reduce oven temperature to 325°F and continue roasting (see chart) until thermometer registers 185°F. Allow goose to cool slightly and carve.

Buying a Goose

Geese are available in sizes ranging from 6 to 18 pounds; most are in the 8- to 12-pound range. Select size best suited to your needs, allowing ½ to ¾ pound for each 3-ounce serving (frozen weight, as purchased). Do allow for hearty appetites and second helpings.

APPROXIMATE TIMETABLES FOR THAWING METHODS

POUNDS	REFRIGERATOR	RUNNING COLD WATER
6 to 10	1 to 1½ days	4 to 5 hours
10 to 14	2 to 2½ days	5 to 6 hours
Over 14	3 days	6 to 8 hours

APPROXIMATE ROASTING TIMETABLE FOR STUFFED WHOLE GOOSE

(Time will be approximately 30 minutes less for unstuffed goose)

Ready-to-Cook Weight (Pounds)	Time at 400°F	PLUS Time at 325°F (Hours)	Total Roasting Time (Hours)
6 to 8	45 minutes	1 to 1½	1¾ to 2¼
8 to 10	1 hour	1½ to 2	2½ to 3
10 to 12	1 hour	2 to 2½	3 to 3½
12 to 14	1 hour	2½ to 2¾	3½ to 3¾
Over 14	1 hour	2½ to 3	3½ to 4

Courtesy of the National Goose Council

Hearthside Picnic

Menu:

❦❦❦

Mulled Cider

Fresh Popcorn

Raclette

Grilled Sausages

Steamed Finnish Yellow Potatoes

Marinated Vegetable Salad

Dark Pumpernickel Bread

German Apple Pancake

Raclette—a term used for a number of Swiss mountain cheeses as well as the dish—is an event as well as a meal. The word derives from the French verb *racler*, which means to scrape. The cheese is melted by a fire, scraped onto hot plates, and eaten while hot. A Raclette meal is one time when it's polite to eat before other guests are served. If you wait, your cheese will get gummy and stringy.

The eating of Raclette was described in Johanna Spyri's classic "Heidi," where Heidi's grandfather, in his tiny cabin in the Alps, melts a piece of Raclette onto a plate by the fire and serves it. This fireside setting for serving the melted cheese has been around since ancient times. Eating Raclette is a country tradition that can be used as an interesting way to entertain.

So why not plan an evening of entertaining by the hearth—picnic style?

Start a roaring fire before your friends and relatives begin to arrive. Be certain to have lots of dry wood in the wooden bin next to the fire so you can keep stoking it.

Spread a cloth over a wooden trestle table near the fire, and set out silverware, earth tone napkins, and tall silver candlesticks filled with auburn candles. Place the salad of marinated cucumbers, cabbage, and carrots with dill on a large platter next to a wooden bowl filled with cornichons. In a bowl, set the steamed Finnish yellow potatoes, unadorned except for a sprinkling of fresh parsley. A large linen-lined basket of dark pumpernickel breads and a tub of sweet butter complete the service table.

If you cannot find one of the more traditional varieties of cheese to use for Raclette, try a big chunk of Swiss.

For easier serving, slice the pumpernickel breads before placing them in the napkin-lined basket.

The cheese used for Raclette is firm, creamy, and mild tasting. When it is melted, the flavor becomes tangy. In Switzerland, Gosmer, Bagnes, Belalp, Raclette, Valais, Conches, Appenzell, and Orsieres cheeses are used. Take a large wheel of cheese, cut it in half, and place one half on top of the other. Set the cheese aside until needed. Wait until you're ready to eat before placing the cheese in front of the fire.

On the hearth right next to the fire, have the stack of earthenware plates warming.

To make mulled cider, tie together whole nutmeg, cloves, allspice, and cinnamon sticks in cheesecloth. Add to apple cider along with dark brown sugar. Have the cider in a large con-

Send guests home with a ribbon-tied bundle of cinnamon stick stirrers so they can enjoy mulled cider after the party.

The discovery of a new dish does more for the happiness of mankind than the discovery of a star.

🍇 *Brillat-Savarin*

tainer along with a silver spoon to absorb the heat.

In the past, mulled drinks were heated with a mulling iron or logger-head, a special iron instrument with a long handle and a bell or bulb at the end. The loggerhead was heated in the fireplace until it was fiery red hot, or almost white. It was then immersed into a beverage and the heat from the iron warmed the liquid.

For a special treat, serve hot mulled cider the old-fashioned way. Immerse a hot mulling iron into the cider, which will heat it immediately. If you don't own a mulling iron, or can't find one in an antique shop, keep the cider warm in a crock pot, or in a cauldron set atop your wooden stove.

When you hear your friends knocking on the door, put the mulling iron into the fireplace to heat it, before answering. Greet your guests with an offer of a warm glass of mulled cider to help remove the chill of the cold.

Serve the cider in mugs with cinnamon stick stirrers. While the guests are warming themselves by the roaring fire, make some popcorn in a rectangular tin made especially for this purpose. Heat the tin over the fire until the smell of freshly popped corn permeates the room. Turn the popcorn into a wooden trencher and serve warm, as is. But if you'd rather nibble flavored popcorn, sprinkle it with a favorite herb mixture or simply with salt.

After your guests have taken the chill from themselves with the hot cider and have begun to relax, get the hearth ready for preparing the rest of the dinner. Pull some glowing embers

© Steven Mark Needham/Envision

Vary the flavor of your mulled cider by changing the types and quantity of the whole spices you use.

from the fireplace onto the stone hearth to create a burner for cooking the sausages. Place a whirling broiler over the hot embers and cook the sausage in a cast-iron skillet.

When the aroma of the cooked sausage begins to whet everyone's appetite, place the cut end of the cheese wheel on cinder blocks level with, and a foot from, the fire. At this distance, the cheese should be ready for the first scraping in about 4 to 5 minutes. As the cheese melts, slide a knife or thin spatula along the cut side; scrape the melted cheese onto the warm plates.

Tell guests to eat the Raclette while it is hot. Serve sausages from the hearth, and ask your friends to take a place at the trestle table.

To eat Raclette, simply dip the potatoes into the cheese. You'll enjoy this dish with hearty dark bread, cornichons, and a marinated salad. Serve a chilled dry white wine with the meal. Since each person must wait until his or her portion of cheese is melted enough to eat, Raclette is a relaxing, slow-paced meal to enjoy fireside.

When everyone is ready for dessert, pull some hot embers from the glowing fire onto the stone hearth to act as a burner. Place a whirling broiler over the embers and heat some butter in a cast-iron skillet. Sauté the apple slices and cinnamon until golden, then remove to an earthenware crock to keep warm. Heat the skillet again and cook the batter for the German pancake. Add the apples and cook thoroughly. Sprinkle the pancakes with confectioners' sugar and serve warm with hot tea.

Even without the Raclette, sausages and potatoes provide hearty winter fare.

RACLETTE

A gentle toasting in front of the fireplace brings out the characteristic flavor of Raclette cheese. Serve this Swiss tradition with buttery golden potatoes and chunks of French bread.

Makes 8 servings

2- to 3-pound wedge of Raclette or
    Wisconsin Swiss cheese
24 small golden potatoes, peeled and
    boiled
2   loaves pumpernickel bread, cut into
    1½-inch chunks
Whole-grain brown mustard

Place cinder blocks, several bricks, or an antique wrought-iron trivet on your hearth, level with and about 12 inches from a roaring fire. Set the wedge of Raclette on a heat-proof tray and place it on the bricks so that one of the cut sides of the Raclette faces the fire. Allow the cheese to soften, then with a long-handled knife, scrape the cheese onto a plate. Repeat until all guests have been served. Dip the potatoes and/or bread into the Raclette while it is hot. Serve the mustard as an accompaniment to the meal.

Country Valentine Supper

Menu:

❦❦❦

Champagne and Fresh Raspberries

Roasted Oysters

Chicken and Wild Mushroom Pie

Green Salad

Valentine Biscuits

Chocolate Ice Cream with Cointreau

Shortbread Hearts

Hearts have always been an important motif in country decorating. Country quilts, tinware, redware, and cookie molds look as if they were planned just for Valentine's Day. As a matter of fact, it is rumored that the warmth of a country welcome is directly proportional to the number of hearts visible around the house. And what better time is there to get them all out than when celebrating St. Valentine's special day?

Valentine's evening is for couples. This is the time to hide away in a special, quiet place with a loved one, or someone you'd like to know better. The preparations for entertaining shouldn't interfere with just being together; so, start early in the day, have everything ready, then relax and enjoy a special evening.

Tonight's theme is hearts, of course. Toss a country heart quilt over the sofa. Pull a table for two to a romantic spot in front of the fireplace or by a window where you can watch the moon slip from behind the winter clouds to reflect on a snow-covered meadow. Place several red candles around the room so you can dine in the glow of candlelight, and set the table with your best china and wine glasses.

The Country Valentine Supper is simple, and most of the meal can be prepared several hours ahead of time. Ask your fish market to open the oysters, and leave them on the half shell. When you get home from the market, place the oysters, still in the half shell, on a small broiler pan; sprinkle them with lemon juice and a drop of Worcestershire sauce. Cover and store the oysters in the refrigerator until you are ready to cook them.

Wash and dry the salad greens. Prepare the individual salads on their serving plates, cover with a linen towel, and refrigerate to allow the greens to crisp.

To make a mashed-potato-topped chicken and wild mushroom pie, add sautéed wild mushrooms to your favorite chicken stew recipe. Spoon the mixture into a shallow casserole, and top with freshly prepared mashed potatoes that have been beaten with some grated Cheddar cheese. Cover the pie and refrigerate.

Roasted oysters ready to serve.

For the cookies, prepare a rich, buttery shortbread cookie dough. Roll the dough out and, using a variety of sizes of heart-shaped cookie cutters, cut out cookies until you've used all the dough. Decorate the cookie dough cutouts with red and white sugar crystals, then bake and cool them. Arrange some of the cool cookies on a serving plate; tightly cover the plate and set it aside.

It doesn't matter if you have more than enough cookies for two people. Cookies never go to waste! You might like to pack some of the extra cookies in a small basket tied with a red ribbon for your guest to take home.

Using the following recipe, prepare the Valentine biscuits. Cool them, then wrap them tightly in aluminum foil so they will be ready to warm at dinner

time. Scoop balls of chocolate ice cream into two freezer-safe serving bowls; cover the bowls tightly and place them in the freezer.

One hour before serving, remove the chicken pie from the refrigerator. Fold a piece of wax paper in half and cut out a heart. Open the paper pattern; place it gently on top of the mashed potato topping. Sprinkle paprika onto the

> *...poultry is for the cook what canvas is for the painter.*
>
>  *Brillat-Savarin*

mashed potatoes to lightly cover the area where the heart shape has been removed. Carefully lift the paper pattern off the pie, being careful not to spill any paprika on areas of the mashed potato outside of the heart. Place the pie in a 350°F oven, and bake for 50 to 55 minutes, or until it is bubbly and lightly browned.

Set the mood for the evening with romantic music. When your special guest arrives, place raspberries in two chilled champagne glasses. Pop the cork of your favorite dry champagne, and toast to a wonderful evening!

Five to 10 minutes before you are ready to serve, take the pie from the oven, and heat the broiler. Place the biscuits, still wrapped in aluminum foil, in a roll warmer. If you don't have a warmer, wait until after you've broiled the oysters and have turned off the oven. Place the wrapped rolls in the oven as it cools. Broil the oysters 3 to 5 minutes, or until their edges curl.

Remove the oysters, still in their shells, to a platter and serve them. When you are ready for the next course, serve the chicken and wild mushroom pie, the warmed biscuits, and the salad together.

Serving champagne in a tulip glass makes the bubbles last longer.

After you've finished eating, remove the dishes and put the finishing touches on dessert. Perhaps at this point, your guest would like to help; sharing the kitchen can be a romantic experience.

Take the dishes of prescooped ice cream from the freezer. Drizzle each one with 1 tablespoon of Cointreau, Grand Marnier, or other orange-flavored liqueur. Top each with a short-bread cookie heart. Serve the ice cream with the plate of additional cookies and, if desired, coffee or tea.

VALENTINE BISCUITS

Biscuits are always best the day they are made. This recipe makes enough for two people (nobody can eat just one freshly baked biscuit), so there will be no leftovers.

Makes 4 to 6 biscuits

¾   cup unsifted all-purpose flour
1½   teaspoons baking powder
1½   teaspoons sugar
¼   teaspoon salt
¼   teaspoon cream of tartar
2   tablespoons unsalted butter
¼   cup half-and-half

Heat the oven to 425°F. In a small bowl, stir together the flour, baking powder, sugar, salt, and cream of tartar.

Add the butter and, using a pastry blender or two knives, cut it into the flour mixture until it resembles coarse crumbs.

Shortbread hearts bake to crisp perfection in cast-iron cookie molds.

Stir the half-and-half into the crumb mixture just until it makes a ball of dough that doesn't stick to the sides of the bowl.

Turn the dough out onto a lightly floured board. Pat the dough out to ½-inch thickness. Using heart-shaped cutters, cut the dough into 4 medium or 6 small heart-shaped biscuits.

Place the biscuits on an ungreased baking sheet, and bake 8 to 10 minutes, or until they are golden brown and feel firm when gently pressed.

Remove the biscuits to a cooling rack and cool 5 minutes before serving; or cool completely and wrap tightly in aluminum foil, then reheat at 350°F for 5 to 10 minutes before serving.

Sugaring Party

Menu:

🍂🍂🍂

Herbed Pork Loin

Maple Baked Beans

Red and Green Cabbage Slaw

Homemade Bread with Maple Butter

Sugar on Snow

Maple Sugar Pie

Maple Ice Cream

Maple Fudge

Sugaring, or sugaring-off, is an event that North Americans have enjoyed since colonial times. Just after the first good winter thaw, when the right combination of frosty nights and warm, sunny days wakes the maple trees from their long winter's sleep, the time is right for collecting the sweet sap as it climbs to reach the sunlight. In times past, the event was reason for a festival. People would gather around as the thin sap was boiled to reduce it to a thick, sweet syrup. (It takes about 20 gallons of sap to make ½ gallon of syrup.) At these events, food was brought in, and sometimes there was dancing. Best of all, when the syrup was almost ready, some of it would be poured on the snow to cool quickly into a chewy, sweet, maple-flavored candy, called "sugar on snow."

Although there aren't as many sugar maple trees as there used to be, and many people don't have the opportunity to collect and boil the sweet sap to make maple specialties, this time of year cries for an occasion—something to celebrate or just chase away the malaise of the long dreary winter. Some-where in Eastern Canada and New England, folks are tapping their sugar maples; in several months the sweet, flavorful syrup will reach our markets. Celebrate that annual ritual. Throw a maple sugaring party, complete with dancing and some of the delicious maple treats you would find at a real sugaring event in the woods.

A sugaring party takes a lot of space. Clear out your basement or garage, hire a country band, and start cutting out paper maple leaves. Invitations should suggest wearing country attire and be accompanied by a maple sugar figurine. Who could resist?

The food should be simple; maple is the star of the party and will probably be the most expensive item in your party budget. Try to purchase maple products from a farm stand, farmers' market, or mail-order source where the prices are more reasonable. You will need several one-gallon cans of syrup, a few dozen small maple candies, and, if you feel extravagant, a small jug of syrup for each guest to take home.

Set up a long wooden table or several tables made from trestles and plywood.

If the wood is attractive, no covering is needed; if not, lengths of burlap, or even beige sheets or cloth will do. Empty one or more of the maple syrup cans into a pot to use later for making sugar on snow, or as a storage container, then remove the entire top of the can (or lay face down and remove the back). Using a pliers, roll the cut edge down, so that the sharp surface is not exposed. Make an arrangement of dried flowers in the prepared can (or cans) for the tables. Using white thread, tie maple sugar candies onto the dried flowers. You can also hide the barrenness of your garage or basement with lots of green and maple-brown streamers and paper leaves.

The day before the party, make sure you have everything you need. The baked beans, maple butter, maple fudge, and homemade maple walnut ice cream can be made ahead of time. To make the beans, use your favorite baked bean recipe, and substitute maple syrup for the molasses, brown sugar, or other sweetener.

For the maple butter, allow several sticks of lightly salted butter to soften at room temperature. With an electric beater, whip in maple syrup until the butter reaches the desired consistency. Spoon the whipped butter mixture into a stoneware crock, then cover and refrigerate it until about 30 minutes before you are ready to serve. Maple butter is more flavorful and easier to spread if allowed to soften slightly before serving.

If you wish, purchase the maple fudge and maple walnut ice cream. However, homemade ice cream is not difficult to make, and is so much more flavorful. If you have an old-fashioned hand-cranked (or even electric) wooden ice cream maker, you might want to make the ice cream during the party. Guests can watch, or help crank the ice cream maker, and will enjoy scooping the freshly made ice cream off the paddles. Just make the custard ahead of time; you can use any cooked-custard vanilla ice cream recipe and substitute maple syrup for the sweetener, but you might need to add some maple flavoring in order to intensify the maple flavor. Freeze the ice cream, and when it is almost firm, stir in chopped walnuts and serve, or pack into freezer containers to store until ready to serve. If you store the ice cream, remember to set it out at room temperature for 10 to 15

Enhance your favorite baked bean recipe with maple syrup.

© Envision

41

Top the pork loin with a sprinkling of your favorite herbs before roasting.

Courtesy National Pork Producers Council

SUGAR ON SNOW

Makes 35 to 40 servings

1 gallon fancy or Grade A maple syrup
1 bushel clean snow or crushed ice

To prepare sugar on snow, pour the syrup into a 4-gallon kettle. Butter the top edge of the kettle. Over high heat, bring the syrup just to boiling, watching it constantly. As soon as the syrup starts to rise in the kettle, lower the heat and cook until it reaches 230°F on a candy thermometer. To test the candy's consistency, spoon a little over the snow or crushed ice. When the poured liquid sugar cools to make a waxy taffy that will cling to a fork, it is ready to cool and serve.

Pour the reduced syrup into several heat-proof (preferably metal) pitchers and set it aside to cool to below about 190°F. Do not let it go below 150°F. Spread out the snow or crushed ice to a thickness of about 5 inches in a roasting pan or other deep metal container. Pour the syrup onto the snow in strips, and allow it to cool until it becomes a chewy taffy. To serve, pull the strips off the snow.

Do not eat the snow.

minutes before serving at the party, so that it will be easier to scoop.

Assemble the equipment for making sugar on snow. It is so difficult to find clean snow that it may be preferable to freeze water in rimmed baking sheets or to purchase crushed ice to make a surface for cooling this delicious maple syrup candy, rather than using real snow. If you are making small amounts of sugar on snow, you can crush ice cubes in a blender to make the snow.

On the day of the party, bake or buy large loaves of homestyle white or whole wheat bread. Bake traditional Canadian maple sugar pies, or purchase apple pies and drizzle a glaze made of maple syrup and confectioners' sugar over the top. Shred green and red cabbage and toss with your favorite slaw dressing; cover and refrigerate until ready to serve. The flavor will improve with several hours of storage in the refrigerator. About an hour and a half before you want to serve, start roasting the herbed pork loin. About 30 minutes before serving, warm the baked beans in the oven with the pork. Set out all the food (except the ice cream) at once.

Folks from miles around can smell the sweet, maple aromas coming from this Vermont sugarhouse.

Spring

Seed Catalog Time

Fleeting Tastes of Spring

Derby Day Buffet

Strawberry Festival

Spring Showers Picnic

German Wine Festival

Special foods of spring, such as fiddlehead ferns, asparagus, and peas arrive in abundance and are at their peak of freshness for only a fleeting period of time. That's the moment when you should invite friends and neighbors to celebrate the first rites of the season, by serving a menu replete with spring's bounty.

Fresh local strawberries are another reason to celebrate. And luckily, their peak of freshness in the market lasts longer than other foods of spring. Have a berry-picking, cooking, and eating gathering to savor these succulent morsels while you enjoy an outdoor/indoor festivity with friends.

Everyone has some friends who love to garden. Gather the latest seed catalogs and invite these friends over to plan this year's garden and choose a selection of seeds to share while enjoying a light lunch.

Spring showers are almost as predictable as spring flowers—without one we wouldn't have the other. And when does it usually rain? When you have a picnic planned, of course. In that case, just move your picnic indoors. A spring showers indoor picnic can be as much fun as an outdoor one—minus the ants.

Any reason to have a celebration is a good one, so why not celebrate the running of the roses—the Kentucky Derby. Whether or not you are in Kentucky, you and your guests can enjoy the race by listening to it on radio, watching it on television, or for that matter reading about the excitement in a newspaper a day later.

A wine tasting presents a leisurely way to entertain. Choose wines from one country, then plan a springtime menu that coordinates the wines and food. By providing a couple of wine choices with each course, guests are freer to express their reactions to wine and food combinations. They'll learn quickly that what they like is what works.

Seed Catalog Time

Menu:

🌰 🌰 🌰

Peach Anticipation

Turkey Breast and Mixed Rice Salad on Spring Greens

Whole-Wheat Cloverleaf Rolls

Herbed Butters

Vegetable Spreads

Kahlúa Strawberry Charlotte

Espresso

E ver since I was a child, I have been fascinated by seed catalogs. Colorful pictures promise bunches of flowers and bushels of familiar and exotic fruits and vegetables. Although there is never mention of the long wait between promise and enjoyment, if the seed catalogs arrive, can spring be far behind?

When the chilly bleakness of early spring is relieved by the arrival of the first seed catalogs, it is a time for celebration. This is an occasion for a select group of friends—those who share your passion for gardening. Give those special friends a call, prepare a light lunch that hints of summer's bounty, and make ready for an afternoon of shared anticipation of things to come.

Tell your guests to bring along any seed catalogs that they have, and any seeds they have saved from last year. The only planned activity of the afternoon will be selecting and ordering a variety of seed packets to share for the garden (there are always too many seeds in a packet for today's small gardens). Choosing seeds really doesn't take a lot of time, and leaves much of

Buy a variety of seed packets to divide into portions to share with your friends.

the afternoon for catching up on the winter's news and chatting with friends you are often too busy to visit with otherwise. If gardening isn't your idea of summer fun, the menu for the party serves just as well for any other afternoon get-together.

Most of the food for this party can be made ahead. The evening before, prepare the turkey breast and wild rice salad; toss it with half of the dressing you plan to use. (Add the remaining dressing just before serving.) Wash the greens; break them into pieces and refrigerate them, wrapped in a linen towel, until serving time. Because the Kahlúa strawberry charlotte needs at least 6 to 8 hours in the refrigerator to firm completely, it is best to assemble it ahead of time. This leaves only the rolls and a few finishing touches for the day of the party.

Think spring when selecting your table setting and decorations. A pale green tablecloth with dark green napkins and, at each place, a small potted plant tied in a square of burlap, sets a festive mood. You may also want to buy a variety of gardening necessities (gloves, trowels, watering cans, a large straw hat) that guests can draw for at the end of the party.

On a small table, set up a tray of chilled white wine glasses, peach liqueur, and a well-iced, fruity Riesling wine, so guests can prepare their own peach anticipations (¼ peach liqueur to ¾ Riesling). For easy service, leave the center of the large table free. After guests arrive, place the salad greens and turkey and rice salad in large wooden bowls in the center of the table,

© Dennis M. Gottlieb

Guests can serve themselves from a large bowl of crisp spring greens.

49

along with a generous basket of rolls and an assortment of herbed butters and vegetable spreads.

After a leisurely lunch, serve the dessert and espresso on the coffee table, and bring out the seed catalogs. Let each guest make a list of the seeds he or she would like the group to buy, in order of preference. Then tally the choices and make up the orders. Allowing one-third of a seed packet per person, try to order enough packets so each guest will receive as many of his or her choices as possible. Then you might want to divide up the seeds saved from last year's gardens. When seed orders are completed, last year's seeds divided, and the winter's news

shared, have guests draw slips of paper from the large straw hat for the gardening necessities. Plan another get-together at planting time to divide up the seeds you've ordered, and another at harvest to admire the results of the summer's work.

> *Gardens are not made*
> *By singing, "Oh how*
> *beautiful!" and sitting in*
> *the shade.*
>
> *—Rudyard Kipling*

A make-ahead rice salad is a good choice for informal entertaining.

Kahlúa Strawberry Charlotte

As light and flavorful a springtime dessert as anyone could wish for, this strawberry-topped beauty is surprisingly easy to make. The convenience of having this dessert waiting in the refrigerator, ready to serve, makes it perfect for special occasions.

Makes 10 to 12 servings

5-ounce package ladyfingers
1 cup Kahlúa
1 cup, plus 1 tablespoon confectioners' sugar
¼ pound (1 stick) unsalted butter, softened
1½ cups ground walnuts
2½ cups heavy cream, chilled
2 pints small strawberries

Line the sides and bottom of a buttered 8-inch springform pan with the ladyfingers, rounded side out. Brush with 6 tablespoons of Kahlúa. Set aside.

In a bowl, beat 1 cup of the sugar and the butter until the mixture is light and fluffy. Gradually beat in ½ cup of the remaining Kahlúa. Stir in the ground walnuts. Set aside.

In a separate bowl, beat 2 cups of the cream until soft peaks form. Fold in the walnut mixture. Spread ⅓ of the filling over the ladyfingers in the bottom of the pan.

Set aside several good strawberries for decoration. Hull the remaining berries and gently press half of them, stem side down, into the filling in the bottom of the pan. Cover the berries with a layer of ladyfingers. Brush the ladyfingers with the remaining 2 tablespoons Kahlúa. Repeat with another ⅓ of the filling and the remaining hulled strawberries. Spread the remaining filling over the top. Cover with a circle of wax paper, then a plate that fits inside the springform pan. Weight down the plate with a 1-pound can and refrigerate the charlotte at least 6 hours, or overnight.

Remove the charlotte from the refrigerator, then remove the can and plate. Carefully peel away the wax paper. Remove the sides from the pan and place the charlotte on a serving plate.

In a bowl, beat the remaining ½ cup cream with the remaining one tablespoon sugar, until stiff. Pipe through a pastry bag fitted with large star tip, to decorate the top of the charlotte. Garnish the charlotte with the reserved strawberries. Refrigerate, loosely covered, until ready to serve.

Recipe courtesy of Kahlúa Kitchens

Courtesy Kahlua Kitchens

This Kahlúa strawberry charlotte will remind guests that springtime is at hand.

Fleeting Tastes of Spring

Menu:

🌿🌿🌿

Ramp (Wild Onion) and Asparagus Pie

Shad Fillets with Roe

Fiddlehead Ferns

Baby Red Potatoes

Leaf Lettuce Salad

Rhubarb Cobbler

There once was a time when late winter meals were bleak and scanty. Potatoes and carrots stored in the root cellar had become wrinkled and sprouty; the rows of colorful jars of fruit, vegetables, preserves, and pickles were almost gone. The only joy at dinner time was the anticipation of that first spring meal of asparagus and new potatoes. Today, we can buy an abundance of fresh produce year-round, and, without the former wait and the anticipation, the arrival of most local spring produce does not create the excitement it once did.

There are, however, a few special foods that, despite international marketing, are still seasonal—free spirits of spring that must be enjoyed at their proper moment or not until the next year. If several of these foods can be eaten together, it is truly cause for a special occasion, an impromptu party. Once you find that the shad and fiddlehead ferns are in, buy them and invite your friends over for a spring feast.

Ideally, this spring meal should be served on a grassy bank beside a rushing stream, but the menu demands more sophisticated cooking equipment than could easily be set up in such an idyllic location. But this doesn't mean that you can't bring the feeling of being outdoors into the dining room.

Cover your table with a homespun tablecloth, then set out wooden place plates and earthenware goblets. Cover the center of the table with a waterproof placemat, and arrange a rock garden on it. Tuck an assortment of spring flowers in small pots into the rock arrangement and cover the pots with moss.

Prepare the ramp (wild onion) and asparagus pie first; use your favorite quiche recipe and add a generous portion of thinly sliced ramps and blanched asparagus. You can bake the rhubarb cobbler at the same time. Wash the leaf lettuce and prepare a sugar and vinegar dressing for it;

The Greeks and Romans considered asparagus a sign of spring and were willing to pay very high prices for this delicacy.

Leftover baby red potatoes may be turned into a tasty salad with the addition of mayonnaise and fresh dill.

© Steven Mark Needham/Envision

refrigerate them separately. Chill several bottles of dry white wine and as many wine glasses as you will need. Scrub the baby red potatoes, and pare away a band of the skin around the middle of each to reveal the white interior. Rinse the fiddlehead ferns; drain them well, and refrigerate until you are ready to cook them. You should try to do the rest of the cooking as close to serving time as possible.

To prepare and serve these specialties at their very best, invite your guests into the kitchen to help, or at least to enjoy the tantalizing aromas. Open the wines in the kitchen for a tasting while you complete the final preparations. First, cook the potatoes in a large pot of boiling water until they are just tender—about 15 minutes after the water returns to boiling. When the potatoes have been boiling for about 5 minutes, start sautéing the shad and roe in butter. Last of all, put the fiddlehead ferns in a steamer, and cook about 5 minutes. When everything is cooked to a crisp and tender perfection, move the party into the dining room and enjoy these delicious but fleeting flavors of spring.

In the vegetable world, there is nothing so innocent, so confiding in its expression, as the small green face of the freshly shelled spring pea. Asparagus is pushing and bossy, lettuce is loud and blowsy, radishes are gay and playful, but the little green pea is so helpless and friendly that it makes really sensitive stomachs suffer to see how he is treated in the average home. Fling him into the water and let him boil— and that's that.

William Wallace Irwin

If you tire of poached fiddleheads, add some to a salad, or deep-fry them and serve as an appetizer with dip.

RHUBARB COBBLER

There is nothing more down-home and delicious than a fresh fruit cobbler. The tangy rhubarb filling is a perfect partner for the sweet, buttery biscuit topping.

Makes 6 servings

⅔ cup sugar
1½ tablespoons cornstarch
⅓ cup water
4 cups sliced rhubarb (see note)
1 cup unsifted all-purpose flour
3 tablespoons light brown sugar
1½ teaspoons baking powder
3 tablespoons unsalted butter
1 egg
¼ cup milk
Heavy cream, whipped (optional)

In a medium-size saucepan, stir together the sugar and cornstarch. Stir in the water and then rhubarb. Bring to boiling over very low heat. Cook until the mixture has thickened. Spoon the rhubarb filling into a shallow 1½-quart baking dish.

Heat the oven to 350°F. In a small bowl, stir together the flour, brown sugar, and baking powder. With a pastry blender or two knives, cut in the butter until the mixture resembles coarse crumbs.

In a bowl, beat the egg and milk together until they are well blended. Add them to the flour mixture, and stir just until all the dry ingredients are moistened. Spread the batter on top of the rhubarb mixture.

Bake the cobbler 30 to 35 minutes, or until the topping is golden brown and the filling is bubbly. Serve warm or at room temperature with whipped cream, if desired.

Note: Rhubarb leaves are poisonous; do not eat them. Trim the stem and remove the leaves before slicing the rhubarb.

Rhubarb is a very generous plant. It immediately begins to replace the harvested stalks.

Derby Day Buffet

Menu:

✿ ✿ ✿

Mint Juleps

Thinly Sliced Country Ham

Angel Biscuits

Burgoo and Corn Muffins

Tossed Green Salad

Coconut Cake with Raspberries

If you can't be at Churchill Downs to enjoy the running for the roses on the first Saturday in May, you can still celebrate Derby Day. Invite friends over, make gentlemen's bets on your favorite horse, and have a traditional Kentucky buffet.

Try to capture the flavor of the equestrian event by covering your buffet table with jockeylike silks adorned with color-coordinated jockey hats and some horseshoes. You could also use a wreath of roses as the centerpiece.

In bluegrass country, the Derby Day feast usually begins with a mint julep, traditionally served in a chilled silver julep cup. If you don't own or can't find or rent julep cups, use 10- or 12-ounce glasses instead. To make this traditional drink, just combine bourbon, fresh mint, water, and confectioners' sugar—there are probably as many ways of combining these ingredients to make a julep as there are folks betting on the race.

While others are jockeying for position in the infield at Churchill Downs as they await the race, your guests can sit in comfort on your veranda sipping frosty mint juleps. As appetizers with the juleps, serve thinly sliced country ham on freshly baked angel biscuits or small buns. Skip the condiments with the ham as neither mustard nor mayonnaise is traditionally served at Derby parties in Kentucky. If a country ham is unavailable, substitute Smithfield ham or other smoked ham.

As guests arrive, ask them to pick the winners of the race. Let them jot their

Need a good excuse to have a a party? Invite friends over to watch the Kentucky Derby.

© Steven Mark Needham/Envision

Serve a steaming bowl of beef-based burgoo for your running-of-the-roses party.

To make an appealing, tasty spring salad, choose the freshest vegetables available from a nearby farm stand.

win, place, and show selection on a horseshoe- or rose-embossed note card and place it into a silver bowl or julep cup set out on the buffet. After the race is over, award the winner (or winners) with either a long-stemmed red rose tied with a red ribbon or, if you want to be extravagant, a silver julep cup.

An authentic Derby Day favorite is burgoo, a southern game and vegetable stew. This thick, well-cooked, and highly seasoned stew can contain almost any combination of meats and vegetables. Some unusual additions to the burgoo pot include squirrel, wild turkey, quail, rabbit, and venison. However, you can use any combination of meats (beef, veal, pork, lamb) and poultry (chicken, turkey), and toss in whatever vegetables suit your fancy, including peppers, tomatoes, turnips, okra, and corn. If you choose to make burgoo, be sure to start it at least a day in advance and let the stew simmer

This three-layer coconut cake makes a spectacular finale for your Derby Day party.

slowly so the flavors can meld. The burgoo can sit on the stove until the race is over and the excitement subsides.

Have the greens washed and chilled so you can toss the salad together quickly. Serve the salad in a large wooden bowl, and set out a basket of warm corn muffins.

For a perfect finale to your Derby Day meal, why not make a horseshoe-shaped coconut cake? You can either buy a special-shaped pan, or cut a horseshoe from a 12-inch round cake. Frost the cake with fluffy white frosting and top with grated fresh coconut and raspberries.

MINT JULEP

Makes 1 serving

4 sprigs fresh mint
1 teaspoon superfine sugar
Crushed ice
3 ounces George Dickel (or bourbon)

Crush one sprig of mint in a julep cup with the sugar and a dash of water to dissolve the sugar. Pack the julep cup with some crushed ice; add George Dickel and stir until the cup is frosted. Insert a long straw, the remaining mint sprigs, and sip.

Recipe courtesy of George Dickel

Pick fresh aromatic mint from your garden to make juleps for Derby Day.

Strawberry Festival

Menu:
🍓🍓🍓

Champagne Punch

Homemade Warm Waffles or Pancakes

Strawberry Devonshire Cream

Herbed Scrambled Eggs

Canadian Bacon

Strawberry Preserves Honey Berry Butter

New England Style Strawberry Shortcake

Homemade Vanilla Ice Cream

Whipped Cream

Sour Cream or Yogurt

Confectioners' Sugar

Brown Sugar

Strawberries are served in unique ways all over the world. In France, a splash of red wine vinegar enhances their flavor, while a wedge of lemon and sugar are standard accompaniments in Venice. In North America, though, they are most often served au naturel or with cream, and strawberry festivals are a popular way to celebrate their seasonal abundance.

At the peak of strawberry season, gather your friends to partake in an early morning strawberry festival. Invite them to pick the berries, then enjoy them in a myriad of ways—from a sweet, fresh, unadulterated bowlful to traditional strawberry shortcake.

Tell your guests to come in comfortable clothes and to be ready to go into the fields to pick the ripe berries. Check your local area for strawberry farms where you can pick your own. If you don't know of a farm like this in your area, you can usually find out by looking in your local newspaper. Be sure to call the farm ahead to verify the picking hours and to make sure there are ripe berries ready to be picked.

If you have a patch in your garden, all the better: You won't have to wait until everyone arrives before your guests can start picking.

Before your guests knock on the door, fill a large punch bowl with all the ingredients for your favorite champagne punch, but without the champagne. The champagne should not be added until your first guest arrives. Set tulip-shaped glasses alongside the punchbowl.

Prepare the biscuit dough and the waffle or pancake batter. The vanilla ice cream should be made a few days ahead of the party. If you're short on time, you should purchase homemade or premium-quality ice cream from a store in town. To save time and make an attractive presentation, scoop some ice cream into a bowl for each guest and freeze until serving time.

Set the sideboard in the kitchen with earthenware bowls and plates, red and white gingham napkins, and silverware. Place a bowl filled with brown sugar and another with confectioners' sugar on the sideboard, along with a jar of strawberry preserves from last year's harvest. Fill crocks with honey

No one put it better than William Butler, who said of the strawberry: "Doubtless God could have made a better berry, but doubtless God never did."

berry butter, strawberry preserves, and sour cream or yogurt; set them in the refrigerator until after you return from the strawberry patch.

When your guests arrive, provide each one with a basket for collecting berries. If it's a hot, sunny day, have a basket filled with sun hats available for those who want them. Once everyone has arrived, you're ready for your trip to the strawberry farm. Try to get to the farm early in the day so you can pick the fruit while it is still cool with early morning dew.

For those who have never picked strawberries before, here are a few things to remember:

■ Select only ripe berries with good red color throughout, including the stem end.

■ If there is a marked amount of green or white showing, don't pick that berry. Green berries will not ripen after picking.

■ Look under the leaves of the strawberry plant, and pinch or pull the stem from the plant. Be sure to leave some stem on each berry.

■ Pick all the red ones available in the assigned row; it's good picking etiquette and saves time.

When everyone's basket is overflowing, it's time to return home to enjoy your harvest. Your friends will have to leave the warm spring breeze and the smell of the fragrant blossoms behind, but they will enjoy the official harbingers of spring back in your kitchen. You can be sure many of the ripe, delicious strawberries will be eaten on the

There's nothing better than old-fashioned strawberry shortcake—hot buttered biscuits, sliced juicy strawberries, and freshly whipped cream.

trip back to your home. That's part of the fun.

Once in your kitchen, give everyone a task to do. One person should rinse the berries that you'll be using immediately, while another should place a whole berry in each tulip-shaped glass. Of course, some berries should go into the punchbowl along with the champagne. Pour the punch into the glasses, and be sure to toast the arrival of spring before continuing the tasks.

Ask your friends to whip the cream, make the Devonshire cream, slice some berries into a bowl, and fill a large basket with whole berries. While

all this activity is going on, you can bake the biscuits and make the waffles. If you serve pancakes, you may want to set up a griddle on the buffet and let each guest make his or her own.

Before calling everyone to the table, check to see if everything is on the sideboard: warm waffles and buttered biscuits, each in linen-lined baskets, herbed scrambled eggs, Canadian bacon, bowls of vanilla ice cream packed in ice to keep cold, bowls of whipped cream, Devonshire cream, honey berry butter, sour cream or yogurt, brown sugar, confectioners' sugar, and, of course, strawberries,

strawberries, and more strawberries! A pot of coffee would be a welcome addition after folks finish their champagne punch.

Guests can enjoy the berries au naturel. Or, with the caps still attached to the berries, they can either be dipped into the confectioners' sugar, or first into the yogurt or sour cream, and then into the brown sugar.

The ways to enjoy strawberries are endless. Your guests can enjoy warm waffles topped with vanilla ice cream and sliced berries, or simply with some honey berry butter. They might also enjoy making strawberry shortcake—the traditional way. Just split a buttered warm biscuit, top half with sliced berries and a dollop of cream, then put the other half on top, and add more berries and cream.

As your guests leave, give them a basket filled with strawberries as a remembrance of your strawberry celebration.

Fresh strawberries will turn a simple tart into a spectacular one.

HONEY BERRY BUTTER

Makes about 2 cups

1	pint strawberries, washed and stemmed
1	tablespoon freshly squeezed lemon juice
½	cup orange honey, or other honey
12	tablespoons (1½ sticks) unsalted butter, at room temperature

In a blender, whirl berries until smooth. Measure 2 cups of the purée into a saucepan. Add the lemon juice and honey. Bring to a boil, then simmer 20 to 30 minutes, stirring occasionally. Cool to room temperature.

Beat the butter until light and fluffy. Beat into the berry mixture, and serve with pancakes, waffles, or biscuits.

Vibrant with color, freshly picked strawberries still warm from the sun are almost irresistible.

STRAWBERRY DEVONSHIRE CREAM

Makes about 2 cups

½	cup sour cream
½	cup heavy cream
2	tablespoons sugar
1	cup sliced strawberries
	Squeeze of fresh lime juice

Using a mixer, beat the sour cream and heavy cream until they form soft peaks. Beat in the sugar. Fold in the berries and lime juice. Serve alone over strawberries, or in place of whipped cream on strawberry shortcake.

Recipes courtesy of California Strawberry Advisory Board

Menu:
🐜🐜🐜

Country Sunrise Spritzer

Fried Chicken

Pork Shiitake Pâté with Pistachio Nuts and Black Olives

Sourdough Bread

Ratatouille

Baby Lettuce Tumbled with Fresh Herbs

Chocolate Chunk Fudgy Brownies

April Fruit Basket

Spring Showers Picnic

There's no reason to call off a picnic just because it's a rainy day. Early spring picnic plans often have to be changed due to spring's frequent showers.

Picnicking inside can be as much fun as outside—with the bonus of no ants or bugs to crawl into your basket or onto your food.

You can create an outdoor atmosphere inside your home by spreading

Daffodils are one of spring's loveliest flowers.

a woolen blanket on the floor of your indoor porch or den. Move other furniture toward the room's perimeter—or if possible—out of the room entirely. Surround the blanket with baskets of freshly cut spring flowers, such as daffodils or tulips.

If you have a garden, try to get outside to cut the flowers before they're drenched by the storm. Flowers covered with the first drops of rain will help bring the feeling of spring to your indoor picnic.

In addition to the baskets of flowers, surround the blanket with large pillows. Your guests can recline on the pillows, while you open the window only far enough so the rain doesn't get in. Then sit back and relax. Just enjoy the sights, sounds, and smells of the misty spring day: the pale purple wisps of mist seeming to hang just beneath the gray sky, the tapping of the rain onto your rock garden and the tin porch roof, and the smell of freshly dampened grass.

Pretend the kitchen isn't in the next room. Be sure you have everything you need in the picnic basket, just as if you brightly and you can be outdoors.

After spreading the blanket, surrounding it with flowers, and tossing pillows on it, be sure all of the foods you plan to serve are prepared.

To make the country sunrise spritzer, you'll need champagne, seltzer, orange juice, and orange-flavored liqueur. Fill terra-cotta pots with ice, and place each one, with its saucer, at a corner of the blanket. Into two of the pots, place chilled bottles of brut (dry) champagne, and chilled seltzer in the others. Tuck a miniature bottle of an orange-flavored liqueur into the basket containing the glasses.

For a glass of country sunrise for the adults, pop the cork from the champagne and pour it into tulip-shaped glasses. (The tulip shape helps the effervescence last longer.) Fill the rest of the glasses with orange juice, then dribble in a few drops of orange liqueur. The children's version can be just as bubbly: Their country sunrise contains just orange juice and seltzer without the champagne and liqueur.

Encircle the blanket with baskets of food. In a basket lined with flowered napkins, have a mound of crispy fried chicken. The simplest fried chicken is often the tastiest: Just season the chicken with salt, pepper, and flour before frying it in hot oil. Turn the pieces carefully, using tongs, not a fork. This ensures that the chicken stays moist; poking the meat with a fork would allow the juices to flow from the meat.

On a wooden board, place a pâté layered with shiitake mushrooms, pork, pistachio nuts, and black olives. Next

Take some crispy fried chicken to any picnic—whether indoors or out.

Courtesy National Broiler Council

were setting up your blanket on the grassy knoll by the pond.

As with all picnics, have a checklist of what you'll need, so that you're always prepared. Keep a wicker basket filled with these essentials:

- cloth napkins
- corkscrew
- plates
- silverware
- glasses

- candles and matches
  (or a flashlight for picnics that
  continue to nightfall)
- cheeseboard
- coffee thermos

You might also keep a wicker hamper filled with insect repellent, suntan lotion, zinc oxide, and a first-aid kit, as well as a kickball, volleyball, and baseball and bat, in case the rain stops, or for those days when the sun is shining

Serve ratatouille as an appetizer along with crusty bread, as a vegetable accompaniment to meat and poultry, or as the meal itself simply topped with grated cheese.

> *"There's cold chicken inside it," replied the Rat briefly; "coldtonguecoldhamcoldbeefpickledgherkinssaladfrenchrollscresssandwichespottedmeatgingerbeerlemonadesodawater."*
>
> *"Oh stop, stop," cried the Mole in ecstasies: "This is too much!"*
>
> 🌰 *Kenneth Graham,*
> The Wind in the Willows

ite herb-vinaigrette dressing.

Line a wicker basket with a linen napkin and fill it with homemade fudgy brownies. Tie the edges of the napkin together in a beggar's knot so that your guests don't discover the brownies before it's time for dessert. For the final touch, fill a flat basket with seasonal fruit or seedless grapes. Choose black, red, and green grapes for a colorful presentation.

Before serving the coffee from the thermos, entice the children into playing a few low-key games. Bring out a deck of cards, a pack of jacks, or a checker board. You might want to set up competitions between families, or between adults and children, or men and women. These festivities might prove to be so much fun, that next time you invite your friends to a picnic, they may wish for spring showers!

CHOCOLATE CHUNK FUDGY BROWNIES

Makes about 24 squares

$\frac{1}{2}$	pound (2 sticks) unsalted butter
$\frac{3}{4}$	cup baking cocoa
2	cups granulated sugar
4	eggs, at room temperature
2	teaspoons vanilla extract
1	cup all-purpose flour
$\frac{1}{2}$	teaspoon salt
12-ounce package semi-sweet real chocolate chunks
1	cup chopped nuts (optional)

Preheat oven to 350°F. Grease a $13 \times 9 \times 2$-inch pan.

Melt the butter over low heat in a saucepan or in the microwave oven. Remove from the heat or from the oven. Add the cocoa and stir until well blended. Mix in the sugar. Add the eggs, one at a time, beating well after each addition. Stir in the vanilla, flour, and salt. Do not overbeat. Stir in the chocolate chunks and, if desired, the nuts.

Spread the mixture evenly in the pan. Bake for 25 to 30 minutes, or until a toothpick inserted near the center comes out clean. Cool on a rack before cutting.

Recipe courtesy of Saco Foods, Madison, Wisconsin

to the board, place a large loaf of sourdough bread wrapped in a large linen napkin, tied in a knot at the top.

Use the bread not only for the pâté, but cut and serve it with a delicious, savory ratatouille. Serve this stewed mixture of eggplant, tomatoes, green peppers, zucchini, and herbs in an earthenware crock. Guests can enjoy it on the bread, or as an accompaniment to the pâté and chicken.

Select a variety of the freshest lettuces and herbs from the local farmers' market. Baby lettuce is an ideal choice. If unavailable, choose a combination of Boston bibb, red leaf, mâche, and romaine. Tumble fresh herbs through the lettuces and serve with your favor-

© Steven Mark Needham/Envision

German Wine Festival

Menu:

❧ ❧ ❧

Smoked Salmon with Spring Greens

Grilled Quail

Fresh Asparagus and New Potatoes in Butter Sauce

Oatmeal Bread with Sweet Butter

German Cheese Board

Fresh Raspberry Tart

German wines are *the* taste of springtime. The crisp, cool climate of Germany, the northernmost European wine-producing country, produces light, delicate, fruity wines that are low in alcohol. These wines are especially good with light spring and summer meals. All over Germany, and in the parts of North America that were settled by German colonists, springtime was often heralded with a May Wine Festival.

While tastes have changed and spicy May wine is not found as easily as it used to be, Germans have not given up enjoying their unique wines with springtime foods. These days, they have just chosen to enjoy drier, higher-quality white wines. For a springtime celebration that your guests will talk about for months, plan a German wine-tasting festival, invite good company, and provide an abundance of seasonal foods.

Select at least eight German wines, being careful to include different grape varieties, wine-growing regions, and quality levels (see "60-Second German Wine Course," p. 70). For a moderately priced selection, serve two trocken

Crisp, fruity, low-alcohol German wines are perfect for today.

© P.J. Valckenberg

(dry) wines with the salmon, two halb-trocken (semi-dry) wines with the quail, two traditional Rieslings (such as The Bishop of Riesling and Dein-hard Green Label) with the cheese, and a Spätlese and an Auslese (Beere-nauslese or Eiswein, if your budget permits) with dessert.

On the day before the party, make sure you have everything you will need: Remembering the salmon, greens, quail, asparagus, potatoes, and cheeses is easy, but don't forget the oil, vinegar, butter, coffee, tea, cream, sugar, and charcoal. Many German cheeses are exported to North America. For a balanced cheese selection to accompany the wines, you might want to include: Bavariablu (blue cheese), Bruder Basil (smoked, semi-soft cheese), Bianco (semi-hard cheese), Butterkase (Bavarian butter cheese), and Limburger (soft, ripened cheese).

Four to 6 hours before the party, chill the wines and wine glasses, and pre-pare the raspberry tart. You can either bake or purchase the oatmeal bread. Set the table with crisp, white linens and a centerpiece of spring flowers, such as lilacs. You'll want the decora-tions to be elegant, but as simple as possible, because much of the extra space on the table will be taken up by wine bottles and glasses. You will need eight wine glasses per person. You may want to rent glasses, rather than go to the expense of purchasing them, unless you have sufficient storage space, and are going to do tastings fre-quently. Have small note pads and pen-cils available on the side, in case guests wish to take notes.

At least 2 hours before serving, wash and crisp the greens; wrap them in a linen towel and refrigerate. Chill the salad plates, and prepare a simple oil and vinegar dressing. Split the quail, sprinkle with fresh rosemary, and mar-inate in one of the wines you are going to serve with them. Cover the quail and refrigerate. Scrub the new potatoes, then trim and wash the asparagus so they will be ready for last-minute cooking.

About 45 minutes before serving, heat the charcoal grill, if you are going to use it. Set out the cheeses to warm to room temperature. Just after guests arrive, toss the greens with the dress-ing, then arrange them on the chilled salad plates. Arrange several slices of smoked salmon on top of each salad.

Open the first pair of wines for tast-ing with the salmon. Suggest that everyone taste both of the wines and compare them before eating. Then taste the wines again to see how they seem to change in taste when paired with the food. Wait to start the pota-toes, asparagus, and quail until after guests are seated and have started the salads. This may mean that you will have to pay careful attention to the kitchen and grill for a few minutes, but the food will be so much more delicious than it would be if you cooked it ahead of time and held it in the oven. The rest of the food is already prepared. Have a leisurely tasting while you eat the meal. Move on to the cheese course and dessert courses when your guests are ready to try other pairs of wines.

If new potatoes are unavailable, select another variety from your local farm stand.

60-SECOND GERMAN WINE COURSE

Main Wine-Growing Regions

Ahr: mainly red wines—fiery, velvety, ruby red

Mosel-Saar-Ruwer: white wines only—lively, racy, fine fruitiness, fragrant and elegant

Nahe: earthy wines, fine fruitiness, elegance, and body

Rheingau: balanced, elegant, rich, full-bodied, good acidity

Rheinhessen: aromatic, flowery, mild (origin of Liebfraumilch)

Rheinpfalz: rich in body and bouquet, spicy, sometimes heavy

Baden: whites—flowery, spicy, full-bodied, ripe acidity; reds—velvety and fiery

Qualities

In general, the higher the quality level, the more richness and sweetness, and the higher the degree of grape ripeness.

Tafelwein: table wine—from grapes of low sugar content; regional beverage wines

Qualitätswein: quality wine—from grapes of normal quality; good regional or district (Bereich) wines; nice with food or other everyday occasions

Qualitätswein mit Prädikat: with special attributes such as:

Kabinett: from fully mature grapes, very low in alcohol and calories; delicate in taste and aroma, distinctly different from region to region

The German Wine Label

The influence of origin on wine is greater in Germany than elsewhere, because of many different soil microclimates; therefore, the Germans have to be very precise on the information given on labels about the origin of a German wine.

Courtesy of Rudolf Müller GMBH & Co.

Spätlese: late picked—from overripe grapes; fuller, richer, more flavor, more distinct; most enjoyable on its own and as an aperitif

Auslese: selected picking—from special grape bunches; more concentrated, very rich and intense; a superb companion to a fruit salad or enjoyed on its own

Beerenauslese: selected berries—these wines are rich and sweet, very nice dessert wines

Trockenbeerenauslese: selected dried berries—the richest and finest that Germany produces; rare and expensive dessert wines

Eiswein: minimum degree of grape ripeness: Auslese; harvested when 7 degree Celsius [14°F] below zero; noble ripe sweetness, luscious dessert wine, very rare

German Grape Varieties

Riesling: Germany's finest white wine grape, very late ripening, therefore outstanding quality; fragrant (peach-like), delicate; mostly planted in the Rheingau and Mosel-Saar-Ruwer

Kerner: similiar to Riesling, more bouquet, less acidity

Müller-Thurgau: early ripening grape for common wines; flowery nose, pleasant and smooth in taste; mostly drunk within the first 3 years

Silvaner: neutral to fine fruity, juicy and mellow; often used in Franken and Rheinhessen

Morio Muskat: very rich in bouquet, strong muscat taste

Scheurebe: fruity, racy wine with pronounced acidity, more body than Riesling; flavor sometimes of black currants

(Gewürz)traminer: fine aroma to rich spicy bouquet

Portugieser: a simple, pleasant, fresh red wine, light in color, good for daily use

Spätburgunder (Pinot Noir): world famous red wine grape, lighter and more lively than in burgundy, very distinct and fragrant

© Dave Bartruff/FPG International

Imagine your German Wine Festival taking place in one of the traditional houses nestled into the bend of this Bavarian river.

Fresh raspberry tart provides a spectacular finale for your German wine tasting.

© Judd Pilossof

THE GERMAN WINE LABEL

Geographic origin, grape variety, the degree of ripeness at harvest, and the wine maker's individual style determine a wine's taste. And German labels provide all the information you need to select the right wine.

What it means

1. The specified growing region: one of the eleven designated regions in Germany.

2. The year in which the grapes were harvested.

3. The town and the vineyard from which the grapes come. (In this case, a hypothetical example.)

4. The grape variety.

5. The taste or style of the wine. In this case, dry. If it was halb-trocken it would be medium-dry. If there is no indication the wine usually offers a harmonious balance of sweetness and acidity.

6. The quality level of the wine, indicating ripeness of the grapes at harvest.

7. The official testing number: proof that the wine has passed chemical and sensory testing required for all German Quality Wines.

8. Wines bottled and produced by the grower or a cooperative of growers may be labeled "Erzeugerabfüllung." Other wineries and bottlers are identified as "Abfüller."

Courtesy of The German Wine Information Bureau

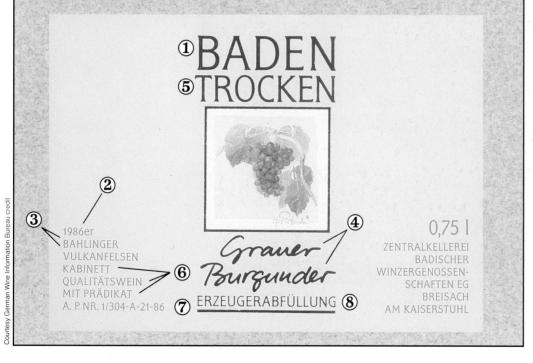

OATMEAL BREAD

This hearty quick bread makes an excellent accompaniment for dinner, but be sure to save some for toast the next morning.

Makes one 9-inch loaf

1¼	cups unsifted all-purpose flour
¾	cup old-fashioned oatmeal
½	cup whole-wheat flour
½	cup finely chopped walnuts or pecans
¼	cup sugar
3	teaspoons baking powder
½	teaspoon salt
1¼	cups milk
¼	cup olive oil
1	egg
1	teaspoon vanilla extract

Preheat oven to 350°F. Grease a 9-inch loaf pan.

In a large bowl, combine all-purpose flour, oatmeal, whole-wheat flour, nuts, sugar, baking powder, and salt. In a glass cup, beat together milk, oil, egg, and vanilla.

Stir milk mixture into flour mixture until batter is just combined. Spoon batter into prepared loaf pan.

Bake oatmeal bread 50 to 55 minutes at 350°F or until the center springs back when gently pressed. Cool in pan on wire rack for 5 minutes. Remove from pan and cool completely, 2 to 3 hours, before cutting.

SUMMER

Old-Fashioned Clambake

Country Fair Sampler

Cornhusking Supper

Too Many Zucchini

Herb and Flower Garden Luncheon

Ranch Barbecue

© Nancy Hill

Outdoor entertaining and summer go hand in hand, and the grill is often the focal point of summer festivities. Burgers are fine fare, but there are many other wonderful foods that you can cook grill-top. Grill ribs for a Texas-style ranch barbecue, and accompany them with hearty baked beans, slaw, and potato salad. Invite friends over to husk sacks of fresh locally grown corn, then grill some and serve with other corn-made delectables. If you don't live anywhere near the ocean, but crave a clambake, you can also do this grill-top. Your imagination (and, of course, the size of your grill) is your only restriction when it comes to grilling.

Gardens overflow with bounty at the height of summer. Anyone who has ever planted a zucchini plant or two knows that at some point the plant produces more squash than an average-size family could possibly eat. That's another good time to invite friends for a meal, and to find creative ways to use the extra zucchini, not only for food, but as containers, too.

Plan most meals for you and your family and guests during the warmth of summer from fresh produce, either from your garden, a local farmer, or a farmers' market. Set tables outside in your herb garden, on a patio or lawn, and do most of your entertaining outdoors. You might ask friends to dress up in their finest whites for a fancy garden party, or to come in jeans, bandanas, and cowboy hats for a ranch barbecue. You can also re-create a country fair in your backyard by holding your own blue-ribbon event.

Whatever reason you find to have guests, summer's weather coupled with the garden's bounty makes entertaining easier and less formal than it is in other seasons.

Old-Fashioned Clambake

Menu:

🌰🌰🌰

Clam Chowder

Steamed Lobster, Chicken, and Clams

Onions, Potatoes, Corn on the Cob

Melted Butter Lemon Slices

Chilled Beer

Watermelon

A SEASIDE CLAMBAKE

Classic New England seaside clambakes originated with the Native Americans and have remained essentially the same for centuries: Clams, fish, corn, and vegetables are cooked by the steam emitted from seaweed spread over hot rocks.

Since doing a clambake the traditional way can be an entire day's event at the beach, be sure you and your friends get an early start. First, collect stones, driftwood, and seaweed. Then, dig a pit big enough to accommodate the food for your party, line it with the stones, and light a fire with the driftwood. The fire must burn for at least an hour or two in order to heat the rocks. Scrape the embers off the rocks, put down a 4-inch layer of wet seaweed, put the food (potatoes, chicken, onions, corn [in its husk with the silk

Clamming is indigenous to other areas besides New England. Here a man in St. Petersburg, Florida, digs for clams at low tide.

© D & I MacDonald/Envision

removed], lobsters, and clams) on the seaweed, then cover the food with another layer of seaweed. Throw a wet canvas on top, and weight it down with stones. To make a tighter seal, cover the edges of the canvas with sand. Then comes the hardest part—waiting about an hour until the food is cooked.

While you're waiting to eat, organize a game of volleyball or tag, or go for a swim. The activities and the salt air will heighten everyone's appetite.

About 30 minutes after sealing the pit, serve some hot clam chowder. The type served certainly depends on personal preference, although certain chowders are characteristic of different regions. In Rhode Island, broth-based chowder is often served, while a cream-based chowder is served in most other areas of New England and Canada. A tomato-based chowder is served in the New York City area.

Once you open the pit, serve the steamed clams first. Give everyone a paper cup filled with melted butter for dunking. Before serving the rest of the food, suggest a fun way for your friends and family to rinse the butter from their hands and faces—a quick dip in the ocean.

Next scoop succulent lobster, sweet corn, tender onions, and moist chicken from the pit. Be sure to have lots of melted butter to use with the corn and lobster, and also lemon slices for the lobster. End this fabulous seashore feast with large chunks of juicy watermelon, and another swim in the ocean for a refreshing cleanup.

Start your clambake with a steaming bowl of clam chowder.

For a clambake, it is best to purchase your food directly from a fisherman.

A Grill-Top Clambake

Even if you don't have access to a beach, you can enjoy a clambake in your own backyard, either by grilling individual packets of food, or by digging a pit in the ground.

For the grill-top clambake, tear off a 37½-by-18-inch sheet of foil and dampen two 24-inch pieces of cheesecloth. Place one layer of the cheesecloth on the foil, followed by ½ pound of greens (kale, mustard greens, etc.), and covered by the second layer of cheesecloth. Place a chicken quarter, a 1-pound lobster, a dozen littleneck clams, a husked ear of corn broken in half, a small quartered onion, and a potato cut lengthwise in eighths. Season with salt, pepper, and paprika to taste, if desired. Fold the cheesecloth lining over the food.

Bring the sides of the foil together over the food and fold down loosely in locked folds, allowing for heat circulation and steam expansion. Crimp all edges to seal. Make a packet for each person.

Cook the packets on a covered grill over medium-high direct heat for 35 to 45 minutes. Open the packet at 35 minutes to test for doneness.

A Backyard Clambake

Here's a simple, easy way to enjoy an old-fashioned clambake in your own backyard.

If you are adventurous and have a spot where you can dig a pit, you can basically follow the general clambake instructions by making a few substitutions. You'll need three rolls of 37½-inch heavy duty aluminum foil, 100 pounds of completely dry rocks about the size of grapefruit, and 15 yards of cheesecloth. Instead of seaweed, use a combination of greens, such as spinach, kale, collard greens; use firewood in place of driftwood, and heavy aluminum foil for the traditional sand and canvas covering.

For a party of eight, plan on layering eight each of baking potatoes, ears of corn, onions, chicken halves, and lobsters. You'll also need eight dozen clams.

Dig a bowl-shaped pit that is 3 feet in diameter and 1½ feet deep in the center. Using a crisscross pattern, line the pit with a double thickness of heavy duty aluminum foil, then add a layer of grapefruit-size dry rocks. *Do not use wet rocks, they can explode.*

Build a bonfire on top of the rocks in the pit. Use firewood and kindling. Let the fire burn 1½ to 2 hours, or until it burns down and the rocks are hot. Do not use charcoal.

Soak corn on the cob (with the silks removed) and 12 pounds of mixed

An assortment of rakes for digging clams at Block Island, Rhode Island.

© Melabee M. Miller/Envision

You don't need to be seaside to have an old-fashioned clambake. You can dig a huge pit in the woods adjacent to your grounds.

Have the seafood, corn, potatoes, and greens ready and waiting for the pit to be sizzling hot.

greens in cold water while the fire is burning. Wash the clams and set aside. Peel the onions, oil the potatoes, and refrigerate the lobsters on ice.

Once the fire has burned down, work quickly to prevent the rocks from losing heat. Tap down the embers. On top of the rocks, layer the pit in the following order: half the greens, strips of wet cheesecloth, potatoes, corn, onions, chicken halves, live lobsters, and clams.

Wet the remaining cheesecloth and cover the food with it, then add the remaining greens. Cover the pit with foil and crimp this to the edges of the foil used to line the pit. Let the food steam-cook for 40 to 60 minutes.

Remove the foods immediately when done. The cooking times will vary, depending on the temperature of the rocks. Peek at the clams after 40 minutes. If they are open and the lobsters are bright red, dinner is ready.

Courtesy of The Reynolds Wrap Kitchens

But when that smoking chowder came in, the mystery was delightfully explained. Oh! sweet friends, hearken to me. It was made of small juicy clams, scarcely bigger than hazelnuts, mixed with pounded ship's biscuits and salted pork cut up into little flakes! The whole enriched with butter, and plentifully seasoned with pepper and salt...we despatched it with great expedition.

🌰 *Herman Melville*

Country Fair Sampler

Menu:

Sausage and Pepper Sandwiches

Homemade French Fries

Corn on the Cob

Funnel Cakes

Caramel Apples

Prizewinning Cocoa Cake

Lemonade or Ice Cold Beer

Remember going to a country fair when you were a child? As you entered the fair grounds, the wonderful aroma of good down-to-earth food and special sweet treats greeted you. There were rows upon rows of booths selling food, those special edibles that you didn't get to indulge in at any other time of the year. As you hurried down the midway, even the dust rising at your feet could not hide the array of delicious foods to choose from. Perhaps you even wished you could stay all day to taste them all.

Each summer, especially when the days get hot and dry, these memories are often called back. So why not enjoy all those aromas and tastes of the midway? If you can't get to the fair, bring a bit of the fair into your own backyard. Invite over a small crowd and cook up some of those memorable foods for everyone to enjoy.

A Country Fair Sampler is a blue ribbon event from start to finish. Send out royal blue award ribbons as invitations and use blue ribbons for place cards and game prizes. Borrow or rent several long tables; cover them with white

© Lynn Karlin

From the top of the Ferris wheel, you can view the whole fair and smell all of the good food in store for you.

butcher's paper, and attach crepe paper (select patriotic colors if you wish) around the sides for a skirt. You could also set up games around the edge of the yard to entertain guests while you put the finishing touches on the food. Borrow the children's ring toss and bean bag games. Set up several candles, and have players shoot out the flames with water pistols. Don't forget to provide a place for dart throwing or a lively game of Bingo.

With the exception of the caramel apples, all of the food for your party will be best if prepared on the day of the party. Wrap prizes, do all the shopping, and prepare the caramel apples the day before. Early in the morning on the day of the party, prepare and frost the chocolate cake (or cakes, if you are having more than twelve guests). Husk the corn, wrap it tightly, and keep it in a cool place.

Slice the Italian rolls horizontally almost all the way through for the sausage sandwiches. Wrap them tightly. Prepare the funnel cake batter, slice the peppers and onions, and make the lemonade; store everything in the refrigerator. If you have enough refrigerator space, you can even peel and slice the potatoes for the French fries; place them in large bowls, and cover them with cold water. If you prepare everything, you'll be free to spend most of the rest of the day decorating, setting up the games, and relaxing.

About an hour before guests arrive, set up a large deep-fat fryer on the serving table, using a heavy-duty extension cord. Fry the French fries until light golden. Drain them well,

Crisp apples coated with melted caramels and chopped peanuts are delicious and easy to make.

These hearty sandwiches have the flavor of an old-world street festival.

place on trays and store in the refrigerator.

About a half hour before serving time, fry sausages, onions, and peppers in several skillets in the kitchen. Toss in some chopped fresh basil, if you wish. Place the sausage mixture in a large baking pan. Cover it with aluminum foil and place it in a 300°F oven until you are ready to serve. Bring a large pot of water to boiling. Cook the corn on the cob 5 minutes. Drain the corn well and place it in a large baking pan. Heat a quart of milk just to boiling; pour it over the corn. Cover the pan tightly, and place it in the oven until you are ready to serve.

At serving time, place the sausages and peppers, rolls, corn, and drinks on the serving table. As guests are serving themselves, refry the French fries in hot oil; drain them well and turn them out onto a tray for guests to serve themselves. Be sure to have a bottle of malt vinegar on hand for the French fries. When your guests have all finished their sandwiches, corn, and French fries, and have had time to go back for seconds, clear the serving table. Bring out the cocoa cake and caramel apples. Start frying the funnel cakes in the deep fat that you had been using to fry the French fries. Your guests may even want to lend a hand and fry their own.

Just before your guests start to leave, you might want to surprise the game winners who have collected the most blue ribbons with small trophies and stuffed animals, like those that were given away at the memorable country fairs of our childhood.

Prizewinning Cocoa Cake

Makes 12 servings

Cake:

12	tablespoons (1½ sticks) unsalted butter, softened
1½	cups sugar
1½	teaspoons vanilla extract
2	eggs
1¾	cups unsifted all-purpose flour
½	cup unsweetened cocoa
1	teaspoon baking soda
¼	teaspoon salt
½	cup buttermilk
½	cup boiling water

Frosting:

5⅓	tablespoons (⅔ stick) unsalted butter
⅓	cup unsweetened cocoa
2⅔	cups confectioners' sugar
4 to 5	tablespoons milk
1	teaspoon vanilla extract

Preheat the oven to 350°F. Grease and flour two 9-inch round cake pans.

Cream the butter, sugar, and vanilla in a large bowl. Add the eggs; beat well. Combine the flour, cocoa, baking soda, and salt, and add alternately with the buttermilk to the creamed mixture. Add the boiling water and beat until smooth. Pour the batter into the pans. Bake for 30 to 35 minutes, or until a cake tester inserted in the center comes out clean. Cool 10 minutes; remove from the pans

and cool completely.

Make the frosting. Melt the butter in a small saucepan over low heat; add the cocoa. Heat just until the mixture begins to boil, stirring constantly until it is smooth. Pour into a small bowl and cool completely. Add confectioners' sugar alternately with the milk, heating this to spreading consistency. Blend in the vanilla.

Fill and frost the cake layers.

Recipe courtesy of Hershey Foods Corporation

North Wind Picture Archives

At the time that this advertisement was produced, probably the nineteenth century, the same tin of unsweetened cocoa was used for both baking and beverages. (Today's sweetened cocoa mixes should never be used as a substitute for baking chocolate.)

Cornhusking Supper

Menu:
🍂 🍂 🍂

Cornmeal Fried Chicken

Corn in the Husk

Marinated Vegetable Salad

Garden Greens

Corn Relish

Parker House Rolls

Assorted Fruit Pies

Ice Cream

Coffee

In the country, lending a hand is a tradition. In times past when there was a big job to be done, neighbors all got together and made a party out of it. Barn raising, thrashing, harvesting, and cornhusking were such occasions. When the company was good and everyone helped with the task at hand, everything was completed quickly, and there was time for fun afterward.

Use colorful ears of Indian corn to set the tone for this theme party.

Today, you probably do not have a large harvest of corn that needs husking, but there are often many big jobs around your home, neighborhood, or community that would be a lot more fun to do and easier to finish if everyone lent a hand. Whether you're setting up a local fund-raiser or organizing a neighborhood clean-up, why not revive the cornhusking tradition and throw a party that is productive and social.

Send out Golden Bantam (deep yellow) and Silver Queen (antique white) colored notes inviting guests to a cornhusking. The real purpose of the get-together (organizing a school fund-raiser, painting the community center, etc.) can follow in fine print, so that those invited know how to prepare for the occasion. Decorate the area in which you're throwing the party with corn, which in August and September is at the peak of its season and plentiful. You can get several stalks of green corn and a bushel of corn on the cob from a local farmer.

In cornhusking tradition, the first fellow to find a red ear of corn gets to kiss any girl he wishes, so you might

Is it cornmeal dipped? Cornmeal gives a crisp coating to old-fashioned fried chicken.

plan to include a few red ears for fun. Tuck the red corn into the decorations; it's not meant for eating. You might want to use uncovered rustic wooden tables, with piles of corn as centerpieces, and golden yellow napkins. If your budget allows, hire several fiddlers or a country band well ahead of the party to play after dinner and the business at hand are completed.

On the day before the party, wash the greens, wrap them in a linen towel, and place them in the refrigerator to crisp. Prepare and refrigerate the marinated vegetables. If you are including broccoli, green beans, or other green vegetables, do not marinate them. Wrap and refrigerate them separately, then stir the green vegetables into the salad just before serving. This way, they will

retain their green color. Prepare the corn relish. Buy all the ingredients you will need, except the corn on the cob. Corn is best when purchased as close to cooking time as possible. If you can, make arrangements with a local farmer to deliver several corn stalks and the fresh corn to your home on the day of the party.

Early on the day of the party, bake or

Turn some of this season's harvest of crisp, juicy apples into a spicy apple pie.

purchase the rolls and the pies. Set up the tables and a covered charcoal grill. About half an hour before guests arrive, fry the chicken until golden. Place it on trays in a 300°F oven until ready to serve, but for no longer than 1 hour. Start the charcoal grill.

When all guests have arrived, ask each one to select and cook his or her own ear of corn. They will need to remove the outer layer of husk and the silk from the ear of corn, then rinse it under cool water from a hose or outdoor spigot. Your guests should twist the remaining husks around the corn tightly to enclose it, then place it on the hot, covered charcoal grill for 15 minutes, turning it once during the cooking time. Ask everyone to remember where his or her ear of corn was placed on the grill.

Meanwhile, if you reserved green vegetables, toss them with the marinated vegetables, then place the chicken, marinated vegetables, greens, and rolls on the serving table. Encourage guests to select and prepare their second ear of corn so it can grill while they are finishing their first ear.

Plan to take care of the business at hand next. Ask someone to lead a planning or problem-solving session, or to organize guests into work units so that whatever needs to be accomplished can be done quickly and efficiently.

Once the meeting or work has concluded, set out the pies and ice cream. Serve coffee and have the fiddlers strike up for an evening of fun and dancing to reward everyone for their hard work.

CORNMEAL FRIED CHICKEN

Cornmeal gives this fried chicken a crunchy coating and an old-fashioned country flavor.

Makes 8 servings

2	3-pound frying chickens, each cut into 8 pieces

Peanut oil for frying

1	cup yellow cornmeal
1/4	cup all-purpose flour
1/2	teaspoon salt
1/2	teaspoon ground cumin
1/4	teaspoon ground black pepper
1	egg
1/2	cup half-and-half
2 to 4	drops Tabasco sauce

Heat the oven to 325°F. In a deep skillet, heat 3 inches of oil to 350°F on a deep-fat thermometer. In a brown

© Lynn Karlin

An abundance of corn tassels blowing in the summer breeze forecasts a generous harvest to come.

paper or plastic bag, combine the cornmeal, flour, salt, cumin, and black pepper. In a pie plate, beat together egg, half-and-half, and Tabasco.

Dip chicken pieces into egg mixture. Place in bag of cornmeal mixture and shake until chicken is evenly coated with cornmeal mixture.

Fry chicken, several pieces at a time, until golden brown, about 3 minutes on each side. Arrange it on baking trays and place it in the oven. Bake 30 to 45 minutes or until chicken is cooked through. Reduce oven temperature to 300°F, and allow chicken to stay in oven until ready to serve, no longer than 30 minutes more.

Long before European explorers saw the well tended corn fields of America, corn was the staple grain of the Western Hemisphere. Its importance is still indicated by the fact that the name corn in English means the most important grain of an area. Native Americans called corn mais, *a native Haitian word meaning "our life."*

Too Many Zucchini

Menu:
❧ ❧ ❧

Garden Vegetables with Herbed Cheese Dip

Stuffed Zucchini

Brie-Filled Fried Zucchini Blossoms

Grilled Salmon Steaks

Zucchini Lasagne

Zucchini Bread and Honey Butter

Garden Salad

Fresh Peach-Raspberry Chocolate Tart

California Chardonnay

There's a time when every home gardener who has more than one zucchini or yellow squash plant becomes inundated with squash. When this happens, that's the perfect occasion to invite to dinner friends who don't have zucchini or yellow squash plants.

Send out invitations with a country-garden motif. You could even include zucchini-emblazoned blank recipe cards; ask your friends to write their favorite zucchini recipes on the cards.

Instead of making all the food for your outdoor gathering from zucchini, use the zucchini as centerpieces, carve them into containers, and be sure to pack a basket of these prolific summer squashes for each guest to take home after the party. Line the baskets with the large zucchini or yellow squash leaves before you fill them.

Use the largest zucchini from your garden to make a container for the herbed cheese dip. Cut the zucchini crosswise into 4-inch-long pieces. Carve out the inside of each, leaving a ring of zucchini and at least 1 inch of flesh at the bottom. Set the zucchini bowl-side up and, if necessary, trim the bottom so the bowl will sit level. Fill one zucchini bowl with the cheese dip for the crudités and place in the center of a huge flower basket filled with freshly cut vegetables.

Cover the table with a green tablecloth, using a different shade of green for the napkins. Make a centerpiece from yellow squash and zucchini, each with blossoms still attached, and set in

One prolific zucchini plant can provide a small family with enough fresh squash to share for the season.

an attractive basket.

Make as much of the food ahead of time as possible, so you can enjoy your company. For this menu, the vegetable dip, sausage-stuffed zucchini, lasagne, bread, salad greens, and the peach-raspberry chocolate tart can be prepared in advance.

To make the lasagne, layer sautéed herbed zucchini, your favorite creamy cheese sauce, and noodles. Refrigerate until about 30 minutes before you're ready to serve.

Also prepare the stuffed zucchini. Cut some zucchini in half lengthwise, then scoop out and reserve the flesh, leaving a ½-inch shell. Sauté some sausage (or beef, lamb, pork, or turkey) with onions and garlic. Add the reserved zucchini and some fresh whole-wheat bread crumbs. Season with salt, pepper, and sage, then divide into the zucchini shells. Just before putting the stuffed zucchini into the oven, sprinkle with freshly grated Parmesan cheese.

Make the zucchini bread and, if desired, warm it before slicing. Serve this sweet bread in a zucchini leaf-lined wicker basket along with honey butter.

Early in the morning of the party, buy the salmon, then stop at a local farmstand for a basket of the freshest peaches. (If your zucchini plants are over-producing, it's also the height of the peach season.) Make the tart in the cool of the morning. Set any remaining peaches on your windowsill to perfume your kitchen for the rest of the day.

Just before your guests are expected, pick the blossoms off the zucchini or yellow squash in the garden. Choose ones that are closed and bright in color. Carefully peel back one of the petals and fill with about one tablespoon of brie. Season a light batter with tarragon and set it and the filled squash blossoms aside.

Once your guests arrive, set the vegetables and the dip outside on a table, put the stuffed zucchini into the oven, and pour some white wine. One way to start the conversation flowing is to get your guests involved in a discussion of their favorite zucchini recipes. You can slip away to fry the squash blossoms, and to put the lasagne in the oven while they're discussing zucchini.

First dip the filled squash blossoms into the batter you've prepared, then into flour that's been seasoned with salt, pepper, and dry mustard. Shake off the excess flour and fry the blos-

Fresh lemon juice and sprigs of rosemary heighten the flavor of grilled zucchini.

As the sun begins to set behind the trees, start the grill and cook the salmon.

Courtesy Alaska Seafood Marketing Institute

soms in hot oil until they are golden, about 4 minutes. Be sure to drain them on paper towels before serving.

Before your friends even have a chance to miss you, you'll return with a tray filled with the brie-filled blossoms and the stuffed zucchini, garnished with fresh squash flowers.

As the sun begins to set behind the trees, start the grill and cook the salmon.

Enjoy the warm summer evening as you enjoy the bounty of your garden.

After you serve the tart and coffee, divide up the recipe cards your friends brought, so that everyone will have one of each. Don't forget to include one or two zucchini recipes from the evening's meal. Tie the recipes together with zucchini-green grosgrain ribbon, and send your friends home with baskets overflowing with their now favorite squash.

Fresh Peach-Raspberry Chocolate Tart

Makes 8 servings

1½	cups chocolate wafers, crushed, about 30 wafers
¼	cup confectioners' sugar
6	tablespoons (¾ stick) unsalted butter, melted
	10-ounce package frozen raspberries, thawed
⅓	cup granulated sugar
3	tablespoons freshly squeezed lemon juice
2½	tablespoons cornstarch
3	fresh peaches, thinly sliced, about 3 cups

Optional Garnishes:
Heavy cream, whipped
Fresh peaches, thinly sliced
Bittersweet chocolate, melted

In a small bowl, combine the crushed wafers, confectioners' sugar, and butter. Gently press the crumbs into a 9-inch tart pan with a removable bottom to form an even layer. Chill until ready to fill.

For the filling, purée the raspberries in a blender or food processor. In a small saucepan, combine the raspberries, sugar, lemon juice, and cornstarch. Stir over medium-high heat for 4 minutes or until very thick; stir in the peaches. Pour the peach-

raspberry mixture into the crust and chill until firm.

Garnish with rosettes of whipped cream, additional peach slices, and drizzles of chocolate, if desired.

Recipe courtesy of the California Tree Fruit Agreement

I remember his showing me how to eat a peach by building a little white mountain of sugar and then dripping the peach onto it.

Mary McCarthy

When your trees have produced more peaches than you can possibly eat or put into pie, turn a bushel or two into creamy peach ice cream.

Herb and Flower Garden Luncheon

Menu:
🌿🌿🌿

Honeydew with Lemon Verbena

Basil Chicken on Fresh Tomato Salsa

Dilled Green Bean Salad

Sage Bread

Large Salad of Fresh Greens, Herbs, and Nasturtiums

Dilled Havarti

Rose Geranium Sorbet with Anise Sugar Cookies

Pernod

Alsatian Gewürztraminer

The garden and yard are a bucolic backdrop for entertaining when the flowers and herbs are in full bloom, and the garden seems to burst with fresh vegetables. Plan to have a luncheon in this pastoral setting.

Invite some friends for an Herb and Flower Garden Luncheon. Send each one a sachet of dried herbs from last season's harvest, wrapped in gingham,

Salvia officinalis, **garden sage, can overpower subtle flavors, so use it sparingly.**

and tied with a green satin ribbon. Attach a white tag saying "Come Celebrate the Greening of our Herb and Flower Garden." Be sure to provide the date and time of the luncheon and add a note asking them to dress in their best Victorian whites.

Plan a menu that allows you to do most of the work ahead of time so you can enjoy the celebration and your guests.

Purchase a ripe honeydew a few days ahead of the party. If you can, buy a creamy white or pale yellow melon, then let it sit out in a fruit basket on your kitchen counter, away from direct sunlight, to perfume the kitchen with its sweet aroma. The fruit will also be softer and juicier when left at room temperature for about three days.

The day before the party, you can do most of the preparation. Start the yeast dough for the sage bread, then refrigerate it to keep it from rising a second time. Poach the chicken breasts in white wine and stock, seasoned with lots of fresh basil, then refrigerate in the cooled basil-infused stock. Pick some small flower buds from your gar-

96

© Steven Mark Needham/Envision

For variety, work some finely chopped nuts into the sage bread dough.

If you have room, serve a garden luncheon on tables set at the edge of your herb garden.

den (edible ones such as nasturtiums, johnny-jump-ups, or lavender), place one in each section of an ice-cube tray, fill with water, and freeze to make flower-filled ice cubes. Make the rose geranium sorbet and store it in the freezer. Season your favorite sugar cookie dough with anise, bake, and store in an airtight container.

The morning of the party, remove the bread from the refrigerator, and let it rise; you'll want to bake it while the day is still cool.

While the bread is rising, pick the herbs, vegetables, and flowers you'll need for the day's meal. You'll need sprigs of lemon verbena for the melon, basil for the fresh tomato sauce, dill for the green beans, and other herbs and nasturtiums for your salad and gar-nishes. Also, pick the green beans, tomatoes, and salad greens.

Blanch the beans, then plunge them into ice water, drain, wrap in a linen towel, and refrigerate until serving time. Make a dill vinaigrette and set it aside. Don't dress the beans until just before serving them. Otherwise, the acid in the dressing will turn the beans' bright green color to a drab olive.

A sprinkling of edible flower petals enhances any salad.

Dice the tomatoes and combine them with some diced sweet onion, freshly squeezed lime juice, and freshly shredded basil leaves. Season the fresh tomato sauce with salt and pepper to taste.

Gently and carefully rinse the salad greens, then dry them. Wrap them in a linen towel and refrigerate. Slice the dilled havarti, wrap it, then store in the refrigerator. (You will want to put the cheeses on platters to serve to each table later on.)

After you've done these preparations, set small round tables outside, in or around your herb garden; cover each table with a floor-length green or white cloth. The tables should be set to accommodate about four people. Arrange white wicker chairs around the tables, and place a natural-colored straw hat tied with a green satin ribbon on each chair. Don't fret if you don't have wicker chairs; use whatever you have available, and tie white and green ribbon streamers onto each. Cut fresh flowers from your flower garden and place small bouquets, tied with the green satin ribbon, if you wish, in the center of each table.

Just before the luncheon is to begin, slice the honeydew melon, sprinkle the slices with a few drops of a melon-flavored liqueur, and set them on the serving plates. You might want to garnish each plate with sprigs of lemon verbena.

Arrange the table seating so that your guests will have a chance to make new acquaintances while they enjoy the company of old friends. You can do this by writing one guest's name on the dec-

Garden-ripe Italian tomatoes make an unforgettable fresh tomato sauce for chicken.

orated side of a place card, and another guest's name on the unadorned side. Lay the place cards, decorated side up, on the tables where you want your guests to sit for the appetizer and entrée courses. Pour sparkling water into tall goblets at each place and add the flower-filled ice cubes to keep the water chilled. Also set out wine glasses next to the water goblets.

When your guests arrive, pour some light white wine to commence the luncheon. Have everyone find their seats and don their hats. Serve the honeydew melon first. Next, serve each guest a chicken breast, diagonally sliced into bite-size pieces atop the fresh tomato sauce, and fresh green beans drizzled with dill vinaigrette. Garnish each plate with a bouquet of dill and basil tied together with a blanched scallion green.

Once you clear the tables after serving the chicken, ask your guests to turn over their place cards and find their new seats. Request that they take their napkins and wine glasses with them. While they are moving to their new seats, you can slip away, toss the salad with a favorite dressing, and serve it in a bowl atop a plate. Bring this to the tables along with platters of sliced dilled havarti for each table and enough silverware for the salad, cheese, and dessert courses. When the salad course is finished, just clear the salad bowls and let everyone serve themselves a slice of dilled havarti.

Allow your friends to sit and chat in the open air while you clear the tables. Serve a scoop of rose geranium sorbet in a stemmed glass goblet, garnished

with a rose geranium, on a doily-lined dessert plate. Place two anise sugar cookies on each plate. To accompany the dessert, offer Pernod, the anise-flavored liqueur.

Then sit back, sip your Pernod, and enjoy the company of your guests, as well as the fresh aromas of your herb and flower gardens.

DILLED GREEN BEAN SALAD

Fresh dill gives this summer salad a Scandinavian flair. Keep a bunch of dill in a glass of water on your kitchen windowsill to lend its aroma to your home.

Makes 6 servings

1½	pounds green beans
	Salt
⅓	cup olive oil
¼	cup white wine vinegar
1	tablespoon snipped fresh dill
½	teaspoon sugar
	Leaf lettuce (optional)
	Fresh dill sprigs (optional)

Wash beans; remove and discard stem ends. In a large saucepan, bring 3 inches of salted water to boiling. Cook green beans, covered, over medium heat—5 to 8 minutes, or until crisp to tender.

Meanwhile, in a medium-size bowl, beat together the oil, vinegar, dill, sugar, and ½ teaspoon salt until well combined. Add green beans; toss to combine. Refrigerate until cool. If you wish to keep the beans a bright green, cool them separately; then toss with the dressing just before serving. If desired, serve on a bed of leaf lettuce, garnished with dill sprigs.

Nothing beats the flavor of green beans freshly picked from the garden.

Ranch Barbecue

Menu:
🌰🌰🌰

Guacamole, Salsa, and Tortilla Chips

Barbecued Ribs

Potato Salad

Cole Slaw

Baked Beans

Texas Toast

Apple Pie with Butter Pecan Ice Cream

Beer

Coffee

During the heyday of the cowboys, a chuck wagon provided the meals for those who worked out on the range. The cooks prepared the food over a burning fire. In the mid-nineteenth century this outdoor concept of cooking translated into the barbecue, a style of entertaining still popular today.

Invite some friends and relatives to a Southwestern-style ranch barbecue. When you send out the invitations, ask everyone to come dressed casually in western togs: jeans, boots, and hat. If you can, help outfit those whose costumes might need a little flair, by providing a pile of cowboy hats and colorful red bandanas.

Head to a local farm and purchase bales of hay to place around the backyard for your guests to sit on, if you have the yard space. If you plan to have a large group of twenty or more, you may want to consider renting a large grill so everything can cook at once.

Two days before the barbecue, make the cole slaw and refrigerate. (I first tried the special cole slaw included here at a barbecue in Oklahoma City. It's the creation of my brother's

A day out on the range will intensify any appetite.

A ranch barbecue would not be complete without a serving of these filling, satisfying, and slightly sweet baked beans.

Is there a classic potato salad? It depends on whom you ask. Everyone makes it differently.

Slice wonderfully crusty loaves of bread, butter both sides, then quickly brown them on the grill after you remove the ribs.

mother-in-law and my dear friend, Charlotte Emmer.)

The day before the party, soak the beans for the baked beans. Combine the rest of the ingredients for your favorite spicy beans in an ovenproof casserole and set aside. That morning, drain the beans, add them to the casserole, and bake them while the day is still cool. Boil the potatoes for the potato salad, then peel and dress them while they are still warm.

In the Southwest, what is known as a dry-rub is often used to season ribs. To do this, combine black pepper, paprika, and garlic powder, then rub it onto the surface of the ribs. Let the ribs stand at room temperature for one hour, or refrigerate them, covered, overnight.

The morning of the party, bake the apple pie. Make fresh salsa by combining fresh garden tomatoes, diced onions, jalapeño or other hot peppers, and lime juice.

To make the Texas-style toast, first make garlic butter. Whip unsalted softened butter with freshly minced garlic and chopped parsley. Cut loaves of French bread into 1-inch slices, and brush the garlic butter on both sides of the bread. Set aside until it's almost time to eat.

Just before your guests are expected to arrive, make the guacamole, using fresh lime juice to keep it from turning a dark, unappetizing color. You can make a quick and simple guacamole by fine-dicing a ripe avocado and combining it with freshly chopped tomatoes, chopped onions, and lime juice. For a spicy guacamole, add cayenne pepper

104

© Robert Lima/Envision

Fresh salsa can be made in a matter of minutes, if you have onions, peppers, and flavorful ripe tomatoes on hand.

or minced jalapeño peppers.

Start the fire for indirect cooking in your grill by placing a drip pan in the center of the grill and surrounding it with coals. Soak hard wood chips, such as hickory, oak, or mesquite, in water to use for smoking the meat. Once the fire in the grill is low, you're almost ready to begin smoking the ribs. To judge the temperature of the fire, carefully hold the palm of your hand over the coals just above the grid. Count the number of seconds you can comfortably hold your hand in that position; when you can hold it there for five seconds, the fire temperature is low and you're ready to begin. Toss a few soaked chips onto the coals, place the ribs on the grill, and cover it. (If you are doing a large quantity of ribs on a fairly small grill, you may want to purchase a grill rack, which allows the racks of ribs to stand perpendicular to the grid.)

With properly prepared slow-cooked ribs, the meat will literally fall off the bones when served. Keep adding coals and soaked wood chips to the fire, but don't let it get too hot or the ribs will overcook. You can keep the ribs slowly smoking all day, until party time. You also can smoke the ribs a day ahead, refrigerate them overnight, and bring to room temperature before coating with sauce and finishing on a hot grill.

When your guests arrive, offer them some cold beer and set out a basket of tortilla chips along with crocks filled with the homemade salsa and guacamole.

When you're ready to serve the main course, add some more coals to the fire, brush the ribs with your favorite barbe-

Steven Mark Needham/Envision

The tantalizing aroma of ribs grilling on the barbecue will draw your guests to the grill, like bees to honey.

Even dessert can be warmed on the grill—just wrap it in foil and place it over the cooled-down coals.

cue sauce, and grill for a few minutes over the hot fire, while brushing with additional sauce until the ribs are heated through and glazed. Remove them from the fire, cut the ribs apart, and place them onto a large platter, and set out on a redwood or picnic table, along with the baked beans, coleslaw, and potato salad.

Once you pull the ribs off the fire, place the buttered bread directly on the grill and toast both sides. Add to the country ranch feeling by serving the toast in an upside-down cowboy hat lined with red linen napkins to absorb some of the dripping butter.

Once the ribs have been devoured, start thinking about warming the apple pie. When the grill has cooled down somewhat, wrap the pie in foil, and place onto the grill. Let the pie stand until warmed through, then serve topped with butter pecan ice cream. Be sure to have a pot of hot coffee on hand to complement the dessert.

> *The word barbecue comes from the South American Indian word,* bar-bacoa, *meaning the wooden frame on which meat was cooked over an open fire. Explorers were impressed with the delicious flavor of the meat cooked in this way and took the idea back to Europe with them.*

CHARLOTTE EMMER'S SPECIAL COLE SLAW

Makes 15 to 20 servings

1	cup granulated sugar
1	cup white vinegar
3/4	cup vegetable oil
1	tablespoon salt
1	teaspoon dry mustard
1/2	teaspoon celery seed
1	large head cabbage, cored and shredded
2 to 3	red onions, thinly sliced

Combine 2 tablespoons of the sugar and all of the vinegar, oil, salt, mustard, and celery seed in a 1-quart saucepan. Bring to a boil, then remove from the heat, cover, and let cool.

Layer the cabbage and onions in a large bowl. Sprinkle the remaining sugar over the top, then pour the cooled dressing over the sugar. Refrigerate for 24 hours before serving.

AUTUMN

Harvest Festival

Pumpkin Time Dinner

New England Thanksgiving

Rag Dolls and Sugar Cookies

Lunch Basket Traditions

Country Breakfast

© Sam Saylor

When the chill hits the air and the leaves begin to fall from the trees, gather the autumn harvest from your garden or from a local farm stand and use the produce as a springboard for entertaining. You could even plan an entire party around one harvest item, such as a pumpkin, or around a cornucopia of autumn's bounty.

During autumn, folks gather outdoors at sporting events, concerts, or take one last outing to the park for a final outdoor meal before the frost comes. Cold air always whets the appetite, so pack more food than you might ordinarily.

On chilly weekend mornings when there's no special place to rush off to, serve up a leisurely country serve-yourself breakfast for you and your house guests, and relax.

On that first back-to-school weekend, you might want to plan a children's get-together. A tea party with favorite dolls and/or stuffed animals is the ideal excuse to rekindle friendships with old friends.

Harvest Festival

Menu:

🌰🌰🌰

**Green Salad with
Harvest Dressing**

**Roast Rack of Lamb
with Garlic**

Grilled Vegetables

**Pepper and Dried
Tomato Brioche**

Country Plum Tart

Autumn is a time of plenty. Larders and root cellars overflow with the fruits of the summer's labor. It is traditionally a season for feasting and celebrating the bountiful harvest that has been carefully stored away to provide nourishment through the winter. As the air takes on a crispness and folks come home from their summer wanderings, it is often a good time to renew old acquaintances, hear about everyone's experiences, and make plans for the months to come. What better way to catch up with family and friends than a harvest festival? Invite guests over to enjoy the last produce from your summer garden or local farm stand.

Write invitations on earth tone recycled paper that simply ask your guests to share your home and harvest. Brown

A bountiful harvest of summer vegetables waiting to be "put up" for winter meals.

and rust-colored linens set with rustic earthenware would be a nice way to carry out the harvest theme. For burnished wooden tables, make a centerpiece from baskets of squashes, pumpkins, corn, onions, potatoes, pears, plums, and nuts. Tuck wide gold, orange, and brown candles in among the vegetables, if you like, but make sure they will not burn too closely to the baskets.

With this simple menu, you'll need to do little ahead. On the day before the party, purchase everything you need. (If you don't have a garden, you'll need to buy vegetables for grilling and for the salad.) Make sure you've ironed the linens and that you have enough dishes, silver, and glassware. If you wish, you can make the dough for the tart crust a day ahead and refrigerate it overnight instead of for the 1 hour noted in the included recipe. You can also wash and drain the greens. Wrap them in a linen towel, and refrigerate.

On the day of the party, first prepare the brioche dough, and allow it to rise. (You can add cracked black pepper and chopped dried tomatoes to any brioche recipe.) If you would prefer something less rich, add the pepper and tomatoes to any white yeast-bread recipe. While the brioche dough is rising, prepare and bake the plum tart (or tarts, if you have invited more than ten people). Select from your garden the vegetables that you are going to grill and also those to use in the salad. Prepare the harvest dressing by adding finely chopped scallions, red, yellow, and green peppers, zucchini, yellow squash, and carrots to your favorite oil and vinegar dressing.

Courtesy American Lamb Council

Roast rack of lamb with grilled vegetables.

113

It is a good idea to parboil winter squash before grilling it.

Several hours before serving time, prepare the vegetables for grilling. Grill scallions, zucchini, yellow summer squash, garlic cloves, broccoli and cauliflower florets, and small Italian tomatoes without precooking them; simply wash and drain them well, then arrange them on trays to carry to the outside grill or place under the inside broiler. Parboil potato halves, red beets, leeks, chunks of sweet potato, or slices of winter squash until just tender, then arrange on trays, as well. Prepare a mixture of half olive oil, half melted butter, and some chopped fresh thyme to brush over the vegetables just before grilling.

Remove the rack of lamb from the refrigerator and rub it with olive oil. Sprinkle it with salt and pepper and a generous amount of finely chopped garlic. The lamb will need a roasting time of about 15 minutes per pound in a 375°F oven. A meat thermometer inserted in the loin should read 155°F for medium-rare meat when the lamb is removed from the oven. Allow it to sit for about 15 minutes before carving.

Note: If you are grilling the vegetables on an outside grill, you can start them about 15 minutes before the lamb is finished. Return the vegetables to an ovenproof tray when they are nicely browned, then reduce the oven heat to 300°F and keep the vegetables warm in the oven until you are ready to serve.

Once guests have finished the main course of your harvest feast, set out the plum tart(s) and a pot of coffee, and allow the easy conversation of good friends to provide the entertainment for the rest of the evening.

Country Plum Tart

Makes 10 servings

Crust:

3	cups unbleached all-purpose flour
¼	pound (1 stick) unsalted butter, chilled, cut in small pieces
3	tablespoons vegetable shortening
¼	teaspoon salt
3	tablespoons ice water

Filling:

12	fresh plums, assorted varieties, about 6 cups
¾	cup sugar, plus additional for sprinkling on crust
¼	cup unbleached all-purpose flour
½	teaspoon salt
¼	teaspoon ground allspice
¼	teaspoon ground cinnamon
⅓	cup apricot jam, sieved, warmed if thick

For the crust, combine the flour, butter, shortening, and salt in a food processor. Pulse ON/OFF two or three times, or until the mixture is mealy. With the processor on, add the ice water in a slow, steady stream until the mixture rolls into a ball. Remove the dough from the processor to a lightly floured board. Knead the dough ball just enough to absorb the flour from the board and until it is not sticky.

Form the ball into a round patty, wrap in wax paper, and refrigerate for 1 hour.

Roll out the dough into a 16- by 12-inch rectangle. Place it on a cookie sheet with an edge.

For the filling, pit and quarter the plums to measure about 6 cups. In a small bowl, combine the ¾ cup of sugar, and all the flour, salt, allspice, and cinnamon; mix well. Spread the sugar mixture in a 12- by 9-inch rectangle in the center of the pastry rectangle. Arrange the plums on top of the sugar mixture. Fold the extra pastry border up over the fruit filling. Sprinkle the top edges of the pastry with the remaining sugar.

Bake in a preheated 400°F oven for 45 to 50 minutes, or until golden brown. Brush the hot plums with the apricot jam. Serve warm.

Recipe courtesy of the California Tree Fruit Agreement

A fresh plum tart can be enjoyed only for a few weeks in autumn.

Pumpkin Time Dinner

Spiced Nuts

Roasted Pumpkin Seeds

Spicy Beer Cheese with Whole Grain Crackers

Beef and Vegetable Stew in Pumpkin

Boston Bibb Salad with Sherried Shiitake Mushrooms

Whole Grain Hearth Bread

Pumpkin Gingerbread with Fresh Praline Ice Cream

A drive along any country road in autumn provides many colorful sights—not only the majestically colored foliage, but the crowds of golden orange pumpkins sitting at roadside vegetable stands, awaiting adoption.

Most pumpkins are destined to just sit on a front porch with a candle highlighting their newly carved faces while trick-or-treaters roam the neighborhood. But that's not all that pumpkins are good for. This mild-tasting vegetable can be used in a variety of ways: The larger ones can be used as a cooking or serving vessel; the smaller ones can be cooked like any other squash —baked with a dab of butter and a grating of cinnamon or nutmeg. You can use pumpkins as decorations on your trestle table along with autumn leaves, colorful gourds, and Indian corn. You could also have a party, and make the place cards and serving vessels from the tiny pumpkins.

For the Pumpkin Time Dinner, tie an invitation to a Jack-be-little pumpkin, then take a drive to enjoy the autumn foliage while you drop the invitations off at your friends' homes. (If you don't

© Dick Dietrich

Use colorful pumpkins not only for Jack-o'-lanterns, but to enhance the country look of your porch.

have a car or would rather stroll in the brisk autumn air, you could make the invitations in the shape of pumpkins.)

Plan a do-ahead menu so you can sit with your friends by the fire and enjoy their company. Most of the foods on this menu need only some last minute attention, so you can make many of the items a day or so ahead of time. You will need to buy pumpkins: small ones to use as place cards for your guests, a large one for the beef and vegetable stew. You'll also want to get small pumpkins to use as containers for the appetizers, and as candlesticks.

Cover your dining table with a burnt orange cloth, and lay out natural or brown woven homespun napkins. Use Jack-be-little pumpkins as place cards.

Carve a name of a guest into each pumpkin, using a canelle knife or mushroom fluter. (The canelle knife, often called a lemon dresser, is a tool with a V-shaped horizontal cutting edge that is mainly used to cut strips of peel from citrus fruits. The mushroom fluter is similar, except that its V-shaped cutting edge is vertical.)

Coordinate your dining table center-piece with the one on your trestle table, matching the colors of the setting on the dining table: Use colorful autumn leaves from your yard, and small pumpkins, gourds, Indian corn, and dried grains, such as wheat, rye, or rice, from your field or that of a local farmer. Place wide, tall, pumpkin-colored candles into the hollowed-out small pumpkins.

© Dick Dietrich

Local farms that grow pumpkins often will allow you to pick your own as well.

When you hollow out the small pumpkins to be used as candlesticks, hollow out the large one for the stew (be sure to save the top for a lid), as well as two small ones to be used as containers for the appetizers. Save all the seeds.

To toast the seeds, first remove the fibers from them. Toss 2 cups of them with about 2 tablespoons of vegetable oil and, if desired, some salt. Spread on a cookie sheet and bake in a 350°F oven for about 15 to 20 minutes. For a spicy flavor, season with cayenne pepper before toasting. Store the seeds in an airtight tin until your guests arrive, you're ready to serve them.

Make the spicy beer cheese with some grated sharp Cheddar or any other hard cheese you have on hand. Blend the cheese in a food processor with some soy sauce, garlic, cayenne pepper, Tabasco or other hot sauce, and some flat beer. (This cheese spread can be made up to a week in advance of the party.) Before your guests arrive, bring the spicy beer cheese to room temperature, scoop it into a hollowed-out pumpkin, and serve it in a basket surrounded by some whole grain crackers.

Fresh shiitake mushrooms have become more available now that local mushroom farms are experimenting with more exotic varieties.

Rinse the bibb lettuce in cold water, then wrap it in a linen towel, and refrigerate until serving time. Over medium heat, sauté some sliced shiitake mushrooms in butter until all the liquid the mushrooms give off has evaporated—about 10 minutes. Add a splash of sherry to the pan, then cook until it has evaporated. You can prepare the mushrooms early in the day and warm them before serving atop the salad.

Make your favorite hearty beef and vegetable stew, and serve it in the large pumpkin. To prepare the pumpkin container, generously brush the inside with butter, then sprinkle with dark brown sugar and cinnamon. Place the lid on the pumpkin, put it into a well-greased roasting pan, and bake for 45 minutes at 375°F. Watch carefully toward the end of the baking time; it is important that the pumpkin should be firm enough to hold the stew without collapsing—the pulp should still be somewhat firm when pierced on the inside with a fork. (Be careful not to pierce the skin.)

Ladle the stew into the pumpkin, then gently stir to blend the stew with the juices that have accumulated in the pumpkin, and bake for 15 minutes at 350°F. Remove the pumpkin from the oven and let it stand about 5 to 10 minutes before bringing to the table.

Both the stew and the pumpkin container can be prepared in advance. Just reheat the pumpkin and the stew separately before adding the stew to the pumpkin for the final 15-minute baking period.

While the stew-filled pumpkin is resting, set the salad, the whole grain hearth loaf, and a crock of butter on the table. Light the candles and call everyone to the table before making your grand entrance with the stew-filled pumpkin. When ladling the stew into each guest's bowl, scrape some of the pumpkin pulp along with it, as it adds a nice flavor.

In place of the more traditional pumpkin pie that your guests will probably expect at a pumpkin party, surprise them with pumpkin gingerbread and fresh praline ice cream.

When your guests get ready to leave, remind them to take their Jack-be-little placecard as a remembrance of a unique autumn celebration.

PUMPKIN GINGERBREAD

Makes 1 cake; serves 12

Cake:

6	eggs
1	16-ounce can solid-pack pumpkin
1½	cups honey
10⅔	tablespoons (1⅓ sticks) unsalted butter, melted
½	cup plain yogurt
1	cup wheat germ
3	cups sifted all-purpose flour
2	teaspoons baking soda
2	teaspoons ground ginger
1	teaspoon ground cinnamon
1	teaspoon freshly grated nutmeg
½	teaspoon ground cloves
½	teaspoon salt

Glaze:

1	cup sugar
½	teaspoon baking soda
½	cup plain yogurt
1	tablespoon light corn syrup
¼	pound (1 stick) unsalted butter
1	teaspoon vanilla extract

Preheat the oven to 350°F. Grease a 10-inch tube pan or angel food cake pan.

In a large bowl, beat the eggs well. Stir in the pumpkin, honey, butter, yogurt, and wheat germ. Sift the flour, baking soda, spices, and salt together, then stir into the pumpkin mixture, half at a time, until well blended. Pour the batter into the prepared pan. Bake for 50 to 60 minutes, or until a wooden pick inserted in the center comes out clean. Cool cake on a rack for 10 minutes, remove from the pan, and cool while you make the glaze. Set a plate under the cooling rack.

For the glaze, combine all the ingredients in a medium-size saucepan. Cook over high heat, stirring constantly, until the mixture begins to boil. Reduce the heat and simmer, stirring constantly for 2 minutes. Remove from the heat. Stir in the vanilla. Spoon the hot glaze slowly over the cake, letting it soak in. Spoon any glaze that drips onto the plate back over the cake. Continue until all the glaze is absorbed.

Recipe courtesy of Libby's Division of Carnation Company

New England Thanksgiving

Menu:
🌰🌰🌰

Smoky Chestnut Soup

Roast Turkey with Oyster Stuffing

Acorn Squash Rings Filled with Peas

Whipped Sweet Potatoes

Fresh Green Beans with Pignolis

Seasonal Greens with Champagne Vinaigrette

Cranberry-Apple-Pear Relish

Pumpkin Pie or Pecan Pie Topped with Vanilla Ice Cream

To me, nothing is more family-oriented, and more filled with tradition than Thanksgiving.

Thanksgiving is the holiday for gathering together as many friends and relatives as will fit comfortably around the table. When I was growing up, this is how my family always celebrated this holiday. In fact, since everyone did not fit around the dining room table, extra tables and chairs were always necessary. I, like most people, associate this holiday with a gathering of family, an abundance of good food, and the aroma of a roasting turkey. I remember the adults sitting around the table after dessert, lingering over their coffee, and chattering about everything imaginable, from the food, to world events, to the family business. Of course, my cousins and I would disappear from this boring grown-up talk to go play.

To continue the family tradition, my cousins Robyn and David Tandy often invite as many relatives as possible to their home for a Thanksgiving celebration. Usually about thirty to forty people come to the festivity, and everyone brings something, whether it's a bottle of wine, a casserole of whipped sweet potatoes, or a pecan pie.

David and Robyn usually rent extra tables and chairs, and arrange these in their living room. Their home comes alive with the hustle and bustle of setting up and serving the meal, the excitement of seeing each other and catching up on the last year's events, and, of course, the children running in and out of the house to play. The day always seems to end too quickly.

If you don't have a traditional family gathering for the holiday, it's never too late to start. Invite as many friends and relatives as you can manage for a special holiday meal. If anyone asks whether or not he or she can bring something, always say yes, and offer a suggestion that will fit into your menu plan.

Thanksgiving eve, do as much of the work as possible. *Do not,* however, stuff the turkey ahead of time. This simply invites trouble because harmful bacteria can quickly multiply in the stuffing and cause food poisoning. Stuff the turkey at the last possible minute, just

If you don't have a traditional family gathering at Thanksgiving, it's never too late to start.

before you place it into the oven. You also might consider not stuffing the turkey, but baking the stuffing in a greased, covered casserole during the turkey's last hour in the oven. An unstuffed bird also takes less time to cook than a stuffed one.

The first course, smoky chestnut soup, gets its smoky flavor from dried chestnuts, which need to be soaked in water to reconstitute them. To make the soup, sauté some leeks, carrots, and celery in butter. Add the chestnuts and some chicken or veal stock, then season with salt, pepper, nutmeg, and savory. Simmer the soup until the chestnuts are very soft, then purée it with some milk or half-and-half. Refrigerate the soup overnight before reheating and serving it.

Make the pie crust dough and the cranberry-apple-pear relish. For the relish, steep cranberries, pears, raisins, and tart apples in orange juice and an orange-flavored liqueur along with sugar, cinnamon, and nutmeg.

You can also make the whipped sweet potatoes the night before. Bake the sweet potatoes until soft; when they are cool enough to handle, peel them and mash the pulp with butter, brown sugar, freshly grated nutmeg, and some cinnamon. Spoon the mixture into an ovenproof serving dish and refrigerate overnight. Be sure to bring the whipped potatoes to room temperature before warming them in the oven.

Make the champagne vinaigrette for the salad; rinse the greens, wrap them in a linen towel, and refrigerate overnight.

Cover your tables with homespun

A Thanksgiving feast wouldn't be complete without some whipped sweet potatoes.

122

tablecloths and napkins in colors that suggest autumn. Arrange autumn vegetables (colorful gourds, squashes, Indian corn) to flow from a cornucopia placed in the center of the buffet table. Place ornamental turkeys on each of the dining tables, surrounded by autumn leaves. If you don't have any brass, wooden, or woven turkeys, ask the children at your feast to make some from paper or clay. The more you involve children in the holiday preparations, the more the tradition and the memories of the day will stay with them.

Set out silverware and glasses on the tables. Don't use placecards at this gathering; allow everyone to mingle with whom they choose.

On Thanksgiving morning, roll out the dough for the pies and refrigerate it while you make the fillings. Bake the pies while you're preparing the fresh oyster stuffing. Stuff the turkey, place it into a shallow pan, and roast it until done. Make certain all the dinner plates are on the buffet table along with a sufficient number of serving utensils for all the foods you'll be serving.

Prepare the green beans and top them with pignoli nuts. Bake the acorn squash until soft, slice it crosswise into rings, remove and discard the seeds, and brush the slices with melted butter and sprinkle with brown sugar, if desired. Set the squash rings aside until you place the turkey on its serving platter. Surround the turkey with pea-filled squash rings and bring it to the buffet.

Before serving dessert, be sure that all the stuffing is out of the turkey's cavity. Refrigerate the stuffing and turkey separately. If you're feeling really industrious, you can slice all the meat from the turkey, arrange it on a serving platter for sandwiches in the early evening, and toss the carcass into a stock pot to start a turkey soup.

Then relax! You deserve to. Pour yourself a cup of coffee, pull up a chair at one of the tables, and get into the conversation. You might even want to inquire among the gathered friends and family as to who would like to have Thanksgiving in their home next year, and thus continue your newly started tradition.

Pignoli nuts add a holiday touch to fresh green beans.

The only known account of the feast of Thanksgiving held in Plymouth in 1621 comes from a letter written by Edward Winslow, Indian ambassador of the colony. In it he mentions venison, duck, goose, clams, eels, corn bread, salad, plums, and red and white wine.

At Thanksgiving, everyone makes room for dessert—especially pumpkin pie.

THE CONVENTIONAL METHOD FOR COOKING ROAST TURKEY

Open pan roasting is the standard method for cooking turkey.

Here are some general rules:

- Once placed in shallow pan, turkey should be covered loosely with a foil tent of lightweight foil, shiny side down; leave an air space between the bird and the foil; press the foil lightly at the ends of the drumsticks and neck; this foil tent prevents the turkey from burning.

- Roast turkey in 325°F oven.

- Turkey may be basted, if desired, to enhance appearance of skin.

- Remove foil during last half hour of cooking for a final browning.

- By this method, roasting times are approximately as follows:

The Turkey Is Done When...

There are several tests to determine doneness. The thermometer provides the most accurate method.

- Meat thermometer inserted in thigh should read 180°–185°F.

- Thigh meat should feel soft when pinched with the thumb and forefinger (protected with a paper towel).

- Juices should no longer be pink when turkey skin is pricked.

- When you move the drumstick up and down, the leg joint gives readily or breaks.

- Keep in mind that the stuffing in a turkey needs to read a temperature of 165°F to be sufficiently cooked.

You should expect some cooking losses. Like other meats, poultry loses a certain amount of drippings, as well as fat.

- unstuffed bird—expect 25% cooking shrinkage

- stuffed bird—expect 20% cooking shrinkage

When the bird is done, remove it from the oven and place on a platter. Allow the bird to sit 20 minutes at room temperature for easier carving; this allows juices to set and avoids stringy meat. Turkey can be loosely covered with foil, if desired.

—Information courtesy of the National Turkey Federation

TIMETABLE FOR ROASTING FRESH OR THAWED TURKEY OR TURKEY PARTS

WEIGHT (pounds)	UNSTUFFED (hours)	STUFFED (hours)
4 to 6 (breasts)	1½ to 2¼	Not applicable
6 to 8	2¼ to 3¼	3 to 3½
8 to 12	3 to 4	3½ to 4½
12 to 16	3½ to 4½	4½ to 5½
16 to 20	4 to 5	5½ to 6½
20 to 24	4½ to 5½	6½ to 7
24 to 28	5 to 6½	7 to 8½
Drumsticks, quarters, thighs	2 to 3½	Not applicable

Remember, these times are guidelines only.

Begin testing for doneness when you are one hour away from completion.

Rag Dolls and Sugar Cookies

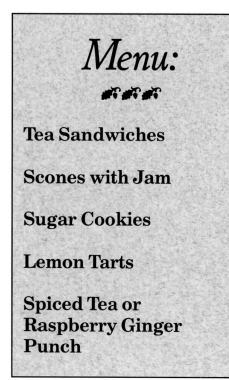

Menu:

❦ ❦ ❦

Tea Sandwiches

Scones with Jam

Sugar Cookies

Lemon Tarts

Spiced Tea or Raspberry Ginger Punch

There is nothing that most children find more fascinating than a tea party. Dressed in the fanciest of party clothes and on their best behavior, children, and their dolls and stuffed animals, can spend an afternoon preparing, serving, and devouring a delicate array of finger foods accompanied by cups of spicy tea or punch and a generous supply of imagination. I have heard of some folks who will serve only make-believe sandwiches and cookies, but that is not my idea of a good tea party and I am sure the Queen would never make an appearance at such an event. So, help your children send out the invitations to their best friends and favorite rag dolls or stuffed animals for an afternoon in the kitchen and parlor.

Preparations may be as simple or elaborate as you wish. Set up small tables and chairs in the parlor, allowing enough places so that each guest can sit with his or her stuffed animal or doll. Arrange pastel-colored placemats, napkins, and a small vase of autumn flowers on each table. Be sure to leave room for a small tea pot, creamer, and sugar bowl.

Prepare the punch, sugar cookie dough, small tart shells, and lemon filling ahead of time. Set out a stack of small aprons in the kitchen. When the children arrive, help them roll up their sleeves and get into the aprons. Then divide up the preparations. Several children can make balls of sugar cookie dough, dip them in sugar, pat them down on a baking sheet, and bake them. Other children can make party sandwiches with peanut butter, sliced turkey or cheese, or shredded vegetable fillings. You can help them prepare the scone dough by adding ⅓ cup dried currants to any biscuit recipe that calls for 2 cups flour. Pat out the dough into two ½-inch-thick rounds; cut each round into 6 wedges and bake them until they are crispy and golden brown. Meanwhile, other children can spoon lemon filling into the prepared tart shells. Arrange an assortment of the treats on serving plates as they are prepared. Place a plate on each small table.

When almost all of the baking, sandwiching, and filling is done, prepare the tea. Heat a pot of freshly drawn,

A favorite doll ready for afternoon tea.

cool water to boiling. In another pot, stir together tea and the boiling water using 1 teaspoon of loose tea or 1 teabag for each cup of water. Let the tea steep 3 to 5 minutes, then strain it, or remove the teabags. Although you would usually go to great lengths to serve the tea as hot as possible, in this case allow it to cool slightly before putting it into the little tea pots. While adults might complain about cooled tea, this will be safer and more pleasant for children to pour and drink. Serve the punch in addition to, or in place of, the tea. Help the little cooks out of their aprons and let them serve themselves at the tea tables. When plates of food are empty, replace them with full ones until the children are no longer hungry. Send everyone home with copies of the recipes they have used and a set of measuring spoons tied with a pastel ribbon.

Scones and tea make a delightful breakfast as well as an afternoon snack.

© Michael Grand

EASY SUGAR COOKIES

These hand-rolled sugar cookies are twice as fast to make as the cut-out version and just as delicious.

Makes 4 dozen small cookies

¾	cup sugar
¼	pound (1 stick) unsalted butter, softened
1	egg
1	teaspoon vanilla extract
1	teaspoon grated orange rind
1	tablespoon orange juice
1¾	cups unsifted all-purpose flour
1	teaspoon baking powder
¼	teaspoon salt

In a medium-size bowl, beat together ½ cup sugar, the butter, egg, vanilla, orange rind, and juice. Add the flour, baking powder, and salt; beat until just combined. Wrap, then refrigerate the dough for 1 hour.

Heat the oven to 350°F. Divide the dough into 48 small balls. Pour the remaining ¼ cup sugar on a saucer. Roll each ball in the sugar, then pat it down to a ⅛-inch thickness on a baking sheet.

Bake the cookies 10 to 12 minutes, or until the edges start to turn golden. Cool completely on a wire rack.

Cutout sugar cookies may be made ahead and decorated to serve along with the ones included on page 128.

Lunch Basket Traditions

Menu:
🍂 🍂 🍂

Green Pea and Potato Bisque

Jarlsberg, Ham, and Onion Pie

Dill Pickle Salad

Black Bread and Sweet Butter Sandwiches

Gingerbread Cookies

Fresh Pears and Grapes

White Grape Juice or Alcohol-free Beer

For centuries, people have packed a basket of goodies to carry along on a walk or ride in the country. As the autumn leaves reach their peak, and the season's sports events lure gardeners from their harvest, hunters from their prey, and fishermen from their streams all over the country, baskets are being packed for afternoons of autumn entertainment and good food. Whether you spread your cloth on golden leaves by a mountain stream, on a tailgate before a football game, or in the park for the last concert of the season, this elegant, yet easy-to-prepare meal will satisfy the seasonal quest for the perfect portable feast.

To be ready for an early departure, prepare most of the food the day before. Prepare and bake the Jarlsberg, ham, and onion pie, and some big, soft gingerbread cookies first, so you can work on the rest of the menu while they bake. To make the green pea and potato

bisque, prepare your favorite cream of potato soup recipe. Add some frozen peas and chopped fresh basil for the last 5 minutes of cooking time. For the dill pickle salad, slice very thinly some carrots, celery, dill pickles, sweet peppers, and scallions. Toss the sliced vegetables with an oil and vinegar dressing. Cover and refrigerate them until you're ready to pack your basket. You can even wash and thoroughly drain pears and grapes; then tie them in a wax paper-lined linen napkin, and store them in the refrigerator until you are ready to put them into the basket.

Who wouldn't be delighted to find this spicy little fellow in their lunch basket?

Preslice and butter the black bread for easy serving.

Sweet, juicy, and easy-to-carry pears are perfect for an autumn picnic.

When you pack the basket, put the grapes in last, so that they are not crushed. Chill the beverages you want to take along. Pack a sturdy tablecloth and napkins, some spattered tinware plates and mugs, and the silverware. Don't forget serving pieces, and a bottle opener, if you're going to need one.

The day of the picnic, thinly slice some black bread. Spread half of the slices generously with sweet (unsalted) butter and top with the rest of the slices. Heat the bisque to boiling, and put it into a prewarmed thermos bottle. Pack the salad, bread, drinks, cookies, and fruit. If you are going to serve the pie in less than an hour, reheat it, wrap it in aluminum foil, and pack it in an insulated carrier. However, the pie is easier to handle, and will keep longer, if packed and enjoyed cold.

When your baskets are filled with your autumn feast, you're ready to set out for your favorite outdoor activity. Be prepared for your guests' compliments as the array of goodies is unpacked.

*Season of mists and
mellow fruitfulness,*
Close bosom-friend of the
maturing sun;
Conspiring with him how
to load and bless
With fruit the vines that
round the
thatch-eves run;
To bend with apples the
mossed cottage-trees,
And fill all fruit with
ripeness to the core;
To swell the gourd, and
plump the hazel shells
With a sweet kernel; to set
budding more.

🍇 *John Keats,* To Autumn

JARLSBERG, HAM, AND ONION PIE

Makes 4 to 6 servings

Pastry:

1	cup all-purpose flour
1	teaspoon salt
¼	pound (1 stick) unsalted butter
1	cup (4 ounces) shredded Jarlsberg cheese
2	tablespoons ice water

Filling:

2	onions, chopped
2	tablespoons unsalted butter
1½	cups chopped cooked ham
4	eggs, beaten
1	cup milk
2	cups (8 ounces) shredded Jarlsberg cheese
½	teaspoon freshly ground black pepper

Preheat the oven to 425° F.

To make the crust, combine the flour and salt. Cut in the butter, using a pastry blender. Stir in the cheese. Add the water, one tablespoon at a time, stirring until the mixture leaves the sides of the bowl and forms a ball. Divide the pastry in half and roll it out in two rounds to make the bottom and lid for a 9-inch pie.

To make the filling, in a skillet, sauté the onions in the butter until golden. Add the ham. In a bowl, combine the onion and ham mixture with the remaining filling ingredients. Place the remaining pastry over all. Trim, seal, and crimp the edges. If desired, decorate with strips of pastry made from the trimmings and brush the pie with the beaten egg.

Bake the pie for 40 minutes, or until the crust is golden brown. Let stand 5 minutes before cutting.

Recipe courtesy of Jarlsberg Norwegian Cheese

A pile of freshly harvested onions awaits storage in the root cellar for winter use.

A cheese crust holds a savory ham, cheese, and sautéed onion filling in this Jarlsberg, ham, and onion pie.

Country Breakfast

Menu:

🌰🌰🌰

**Bran Flakes
Muesli**

**Flaked Coconut,
Sesame Seeds,
Sunflower Seeds**

**Golden Raisins, Raisins,
Unsalted Hazelnuts**

Orange Juice

Milk

Seasonal Fruit

Soft Cooked Eggs

**Sliced Meats, Sliced
Cheeses**

**Pumpernickel, Rye,
Wheatberry Breads**

Homemade Preserves

During the week, breakfast is usually rushed. You often just grab a cup of coffee and a slice of toast on the way to work. Weekends should be different; this is the time to relax and linger over a country breakfast, have an extra cup of coffee, and enjoy the company of family and weekend guests. Instead of waiting until everyone's awake, set out a buffet breakfast bar, where guests can help themselves whenever they're ready to eat. This will minimize your time in the kitchen, and will make it possible for you to have a leisurely chat with each guest as he or she comes down for breakfast.

Set the buffet near a window where the early morning sun will sparkle on the juice pitchers and illuminate all the delicious foods set out on the buffet. Use a crisp white linen tablecloth to cover the buffet table, or if you have a tiled topped table, leave it unadorned. Look around your home for breakfast trinkets (brass roosters, chicken-shaped baskets, egg-shaped ornaments) to decorate the table. You may want to add small baskets of autumn flowers, too.

Form rosebuds from crisp white linen napkins and arrange them on the small tables that you've set around your porch or other sunny room. Fill a tiny vase with a flower bud for a centerpiece on each table. If you have them, set colorful Fiestaware or other brightly colored luncheon plates, cups and saucers, sugar bowls, cream pitchers, and bread plates on the table.

With a butter curler, make ribbed cowrie-shell shapes of butter. (A butter curler is a serrated blade, curved like a shepherd's crook.) To make the curls, scrape the butter curler across the top of a chilled block of butter. As you do this, dip the curler in a glass of hot water from time to time, but keep the butter and curls cool. Fill a silver dish with the curls, and store it in the refrigerator until your guests sit down.

Nestle three jelly jars in a crisp white napkin on a plate. Fill each jar with a different flavor of homemade preserves.

Set up the breakfast bar with as many unusual cereal items as possible. Fill large apothecary or Mason jars with ingredients that your guests can combine for a nourishing breakfast cereal. Include bran flakes, homemade muesli, sesame seeds, sunflower seeds, flaked

n abundance of whole grain breads awaits the arrival of the first breakfast guest.

Guests may create their own favorite breakfast from an assortment of seasonal fruit, yogurts, and toppings.

coconut, raisins, and unsalted hazelnuts. Fill a bowl with fruits of the season: orange and grapefruit segments, and sliced apples and sliced pears in a citrus bath.

Add a platter of cheeses and sliced meat and a huge bread basket assortment, such as muffins, biscuits, sour seeded rye bread, pumpernickel bread, and whole grain rolls.

Set glass pitchers full of orange juice, grapefruit juice, and water on white porcelain doily-lined plates to catch their condensation. Store a glass pitcher of milk in the refrigerator.

Provide plain and flavored yogurts to top the muesli. If you have the time and inclination, make the yogurt.

Place a woven pottery basket (or a ceramic tile) into a 350°F oven for about 15 minutes to warm it. Line the basket with a linen napkin and fill it with warm soft-cooked eggs. If you use a tile, place it into an egg cozy, then fill with the eggs. Those who rise first will have soft-cooked eggs; the late risers will find hard-cooked ones, since the eggs will continue to cook.

The last item for the buffet is, of course, freshly brewed hot coffee. Store the cream and milk in the refrigerator and position a note to that effect on the buffet. You may also want to serve tea; if so, put an assortment of tea bags in a small basket on the table, and some lemon wedges, and let your guests boil their water in the kitchen.

Provide a stack of morning papers for leisurely reading, and let your guests rise when they wish, then enjoy an unhurried, sumptuous country breakfast.

© Margerine St./FPG International

Warm, soft-cooked eggs provide a country welcome at breakfast.

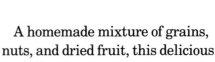

MUESLI

A homemade mixture of grains, nuts, and dried fruit, this delicious breakfast-in-a-bowl can be anything you want it to be. The following recipe is just a suggestion; add your favorite fruit, nuts, or seeds and make it different every time.

Makes about 2 quarts dry cereal; serves 8

3	cups old-fashioned rolled oats
1½	cups rolled wheat or barley
1	cup flaked corn or wheat cereal
½	cup oat bran
½	cup sliced natural almonds
½	cup slivered dried apricots
½	cup chopped dried dates
½	cup seedless raisins
¼	cup chopped hazelnuts or walnuts
¼	cup sesame seeds
¼	cup wheat germ
¼	cup sunflower kernels
¼	cup light brown sugar (optional)

Milk or yogurt

In a large bowl, combine all the ingredients, except the milk or yogurt. Store the muesli in airtight containers until ready to use. Serve the muesli with milk or yogurt. If desired, combine the muesli and milk or yogurt several hours ahead of time and refrigerate until ready to serve. A creamy cereal will result.

COOKWARE AND BAKEWARE EQUIVALENTS

BAKEWARE	DIMENSIONS		VOLUME	
	Imperial	Metric	Imperial	Metric
Round Layer Cake Pans	8 × 1-1/2-inch	20 × 4 cm	5 cups	1.2 L
	9 × 1-3/8-inch	22 × 3.5 cm	6 cups	1.5 L
Square Cake Pans	8 × 8 × 2-inch	20 × 20 × 5 cm	8 cups	2 L
	9 × 9 × 1-3/4-inch	23 × 23 × 4.5 cm	10 cups	2.5 L
Square Fruitcake Pans	6 × 6 × 3-inch	15 × 15 × 8 cm	8 cups	2 L
	7 × 7 × 3-inch	18 × 18 × 8 cm	10 cups	2.5 L
	8 × 8 × 3-inch	20 × 20 × 8 cm	12 cups	3 L
Baking Dishes	11 × 7 × 1-1/2-inch	28 × 18 × 4 cm	8 cups	2 L
	12 × 8 × 1-3/4-inch	30 × 20 × 4.5 cm	12 cups	3 L
	13 × 9 × 2-inch	33 × 23 × 5 cm	14 cups	3.5 L
Loaf Pans	8-1/2 × 4-1/2 × 2-1/2-inch	22 × 11 × 6 cm	6 cups	1.5 L
	9 × 5 × 2-1/2-inch	23 × 13 × 6 cm	8 cups	2 L
Springform Pans	8 × 2-1/2-inch	20 × 6 cm	8 cups	2 L
	9 × 2-1/2-inch	23 × 6 cm	10 cups	2.5 L
	10 × 2-1/2-inch	25 × 6 cm	12 cups	3 L
Tube Pans	9 × 4-inch	23 × 10 cm	12 cups	3 L
	10 × 4-1/2-inch	25 × 11 cm	16 cups	4 L
Bundt Pan	10 × 3-3/4-inch	25 × 9.5 cm	12 cups	3 L
Jelly Roll Pans	15-1/2 × 10-1/2 × 3/4-inch	39 × 27 × 2 cm	8 cups	2 L
	17-1/2 × 11-1/2 × 3/4-inch	45 × 29 × 2 cm	12 cups	3 L
Pie Plates	8 × 1-1/2-inch	20 × 4 cm	3 cups	750 mL
or	9 × 1-1/2-inch	23 × 4 cm	4 cups	1 L
Flan Pans	10 × 1-3/4-inch	25 × 4.5 cm	6 cups	1.5 L
Soufflé Dishes	7 × 3-inch	18 × 8 cm	6 cups	1.5 L
	8 × 3-3/4-inch	20 × 9.5 cm	10 cups	2.5 L
Ring Moulds	8-1/2 × 1-3/4-inch	22 × 4.5 cm	4 cups	1 L
	9-1/2 × 2-inch	24 × 5 cm	6 cups	1.5 L
Muffin Cups	2-3/4 × 1-inch	7 × 2.5 cm	1/3 cup	75 mL
	2-3/4 × 1-1/4-inch	7 × 3.2 cm	1/2 cup	125 mL
Custard Cups	3 × 1-1/2-inch	8 × 4 cm	1/2 cup	125 mL
	3-1/2 × 1-3/4-inch	9 × 4.5 cm	3/4 cup	175 mL

WEIGHT AND VOLUME EQUIVALENTS (APPROXIMATE) – VEGETABLES

VEGETABLE	WEIGHT	VOLUME	NUMBER
Asparagus	1 lb (500 g)	4 cups (1 L) 1-inch (2.5-cm) pieces	16 to 20 medium spears
Beans, Green or Wax	1 lb (500 g)	3 cups (750 mL) 1-inch (2.5-cm) pieces	
Beets	1 lb (500 g)	2 cups (500 mL) diced	3 medium
Broccoli	1 lb (500 g)	3½ cups (875 mL) florets	1 medium bunch
Cabbage	2 lb (1 kg)	8 cups (2 L) shredded	1 medium head
Carrots	1 lb (500 g)	3 cups (750 mL) sliced or shredded	5 to 6 medium
Cauliflower	2 lb (1 kg)	4 cups (1 L) florets	1 large head
Celery	¼ lb (125 g)	1 cup (250 mL) sliced	2 stalks
Cucumber, Field	½ lb (250 g)	2 cups (500 mL) sliced or diced	1 medium
Cucumber, Pickling	1 lb (500 g)	2½ cups (625 mL) sliced	5 medium
Eggplant	1 lb (500 g)	2½ cups (625 mL) diced	1 medium
Green Onions	¼ lb (125 g)	½ cup (125 mL) sliced	1 bunch, 8 medium
Lettuce, Boston	½ lb (250g)	6 cups (1.5 L) bite-size pieces	1 small head
Lettuce, Iceberg	1¼ lb (625g)	6 cups (1.5 L) shredded 10 cups (2.5 L) bite-size pieces	1 small head
Mushrooms	½ lb (250 g)	3 cups (750 mL) sliced	24 medium
Onions, Cooking	1 lb (500 g)	2 cups (500 mL) chopped 3 cups (750 mL) sliced	5 medium
Onions, Spanish	1¼ lb (625 g)	3 cups (750 mL) chopped 4 cups (1 L) sliced	1
Potatoes, Baking	1 lb (500 g)	4 cups (1 L) sliced or diced 1¾ cups (425 mL) mashed	3 medium
Potatoes, New	1 lb (500 g)	4 cups (1 L) sliced or diced	7 medium
Peppers, Green, Red, Sweet, or Yellow	1 lb (500 g)	2 cups (500 mL) chopped	2 large
Radishes	¼ lb (125 g)	1 cup (250 mL) sliced	12 medium
Rutabaga	2 lb (1 kg)	4 cups (1 L) diced	1 large
Spinach	10 oz (284 g)	6 cups (1.5 L) torn 1½ cups (375 mL) cooked	
Tomatoes	1 lb (500 g)	3 cups (750 mL) chopped	3 medium
Turnip, White	1 lb (500 g)	3 cups (750 mL) cubed	4 medium
Zucchini	1 lb (500 g)	3 cups (750 mL) sliced	3 to 4 medium

WEIGHT AND VOLUME EQUIVALENTS (APPROXIMATE) – FRUITS

FRUIT	WEIGHT	VOLUME	NUMBER
Apples	1 lb (500 g)	3 cups (750 mL) chopped 4 cups (1 L) sliced	3 medium
Apricots	1 lb (500 g)	2¼ cups (550 mL) chopped	8 to 12 medium
Bananas	1 lb (500 g)	2 cups (500 mL) sliced 1⅓ cups (325 mL) mashed	3 medium
Black Currants	1 lb (500 g)	3 cups (750 mL) whole	
Blueberries	1 lb (500 g)	3 cups (750 mL) whole 2½ cups (625 mL) lightly crushed	
Cherries	1 lb (500 g)	2½ cups (625 mL) whole	
Cranberries	¾ lb (375 g)	3 cups (750 mL) whole	
Gooseberries	1 lb (500 g)	4 cups (1 L) whole	
Grapes	1 lb (500 g)	2½ cups (625 mL) whole	
Lemons	6 oz (175 g)	⅓ cup (75 mL) juice	1 medium
Limes	3 oz (75 g)	3 tbsp (50 mL) juice	1 medium
Melons (Honeydew)	4 lb (2 kg)	4 cups (1 L) balls	1 medium
Melons (Cantaloupe)	2 lb (1 kg)	2 cups (500 mL) balls	1 medium
Oranges	½ lb (250 g)	½ cup (125 mL) juice	1 medium
Peaches	1 lb (500 g)	1½ cups (375 mL) chopped 2 cups (500 mL) sliced	4 medium
Pears	1 lb (500 g)	2½ cups (625 mL) chopped 3 cups (750 mL) sliced	4 medium
Pineapple	2 lb (1 kg)	3 cups (750 mL) 1-inch (2.5-cm) cubes	1 medium
Plums	1 lb (500 g)	2½ cups (625 mL) pitted and chopped	8 to 12 medium
Raspberries	1 lb (500 g)	4 cups (1 L) whole 2 cups (500 mL) lightly crushed	
Rhubarb	1 lb (500 g)	3 cups (750 mL) 1-inch (2.5-cm) pieces	4 to 8 stalks
Strawberries	1 lb (500 g)	4 cups (1 L) whole 2 cups (500 mL) lightly crushed	

KITCHEN METRICS

For cooking and baking convenience, we suggest that you use the following table for adapting to metric measurement. The table gives approximate, rather than exact, conversions.

SPOONS

¼ teaspoon   = 1 milliliter
½ teaspoon   = 2 milliliters
1 teaspoon   = 5 milliliters
1 tablespoon = 15 milliliters
2 tablespoons = 25 milliliters
3 tablespoons = 50 milliliters

CUPS

¼ cup   = 50 milliliters
⅓ cup   = 75 milliliters
½ cup   = 125 milliliters
⅔ cup   = 150 milliliters
¾ cup   = 175 milliliters
1 cup   = 250 milliliters
1 pint = 500 milliliters
1 quart = .95 liters
1 gallon = 3.8 liters

TO ADAPT LENGTHS

one inch = 2.5 centimeters
one foot = 30 centimeters
one yard = .9 meters

OVEN TEMPERATURES

200°F = 100°C
225°F = 110°C
250°F = 120°C
275°F = 140°C
300°F = 150°C
325°F = 160°C
350°F = 180°C
375°F = 190°C
400°F = 200°C
425°F = 220°C
450°F = 230°C
475°F = 240°C

TO ADAPT WEIGHTS

one ounce = 28 grams
one pound = .45 kilograms

© Jeff Greenberg

Index

Main entries in **boldface** indicate recipes. Foods and dishes in regular type are discussed within their respective chapters; however, actual recipes are not given.

A

Acorn squash, 120–25
Angel biscuits, 56–59
Apple pancake, 30–35
Apple pie, 102–7
Apple pie with cinnamon ice cream, 24–29
Apples
  caramel, 84–87
  sweet potatoes with, 24–29
Asparagus, and ramp pie, 52–55
Avocado salad, 16–19

B

Baked beans, 40–43, 102–7
Baked Beef and Mushroom Stew, 22
Barbecued ribs, 102–7
Bartlett Pear Squares, 19
Basil chicken, 96–101
Beans
  baked, 102–7
  dilled green bean salad, 101
  green, 120–25
  maple baked, 40–43
Beef
  and mushroom stew, 22
  and vegetable stew, 116–19
Beer, 16–19, 78–83, 84–87, 102–7
Biscuits
  angel, 56–59
  hot buttered, 20–23
  Valentine, 39

Black bread and sweet butter sandwiches, 130–33
Boston bibb salad, 116–19
Breads
  cloverleaf rolls, 48–51
  corn, 16–19
  corn muffins, 56–59
  hot buttered biscuits, 20–23
  with maple butter, 40–43
  oatmeal, 73
  Parker house rolls, 24–29
  pumpernickel, 30–35, 134–37
  rye, 134–37
  sage, 96–101
  sourdough, 64–67
  wheatberry, 134–37
  whole grain hearth, 116–19
  zucchini, 92–95
Brownies, chocolate chunk fudgy, 67
Burgoo and corn muffins, 56–59
Buttered biscuits, 20–23
Butters
  honey berry, 63
  maple, 40–43

C

Cabbage
  cole slaw, 107
  red and green slaw, 40–43
Cakes
  chocolate chunk fudgy brownies, 67
  cocoa, 87
  coconut with raspberries, 56–59
  funnel, 84–87
  strawberry shortcake, 60–63
Canadian bacon, 60–63
Candied sweet potatoes with apples, 24–29
Caramel apples, 84–87
Cereals, muesli, 137
Champagne and raspberries, 36–39
Champagne punch, 60–63

Charlotte Emmer's Special Cole Slaw, 107
Cheese
  and ham and onion pie, 132
  dilled havarti, 96–101
  herbed dip, 92–95
  Raclette, 35
  sliced, 134–37
  spicy beer, 116–19
Chestnut soup, 120–25
Chestnut stuffing, 24–29
Chicken
  basil, 96–101
  fried, 64–67, 91
  pie with mushrooms, 36–39
Chili, beef and chicken, 16–19
Chocolate Chunk Fudgy Brownies, 67
Chocolate ice cream with Cointreau, 36–39
Chocolate tart, peach-raspberry, 94
Cider
  chilled, 16–19
  mulled, 30–35
Clambakes, 81–83
Clam chowder, 78–83
Cloverleaf rolls, 48–51
Cobblers, rhubarb, 55
Cocoa cake, 87
Coconut, flaked, 134–37
Coconut cake with raspberries, 56–59
Coffee, 20–23, 24–29, 88–91, 102–7
  espresso, 48–51
Cointreau, chocolate ice cream with, 36–39
Cole slaw, 107
Cookies
  gingerbread, 130–33
  sugar, 128
Corn bread, 16–19
Corn in the husk, 88–91
Cornmeal Fried Chicken, 91
Corn muffins, burgoo and, 56–59
Corn on the cob, 84–87
Corn relish, 88–91

Country Plum Tart, 114
Cranberry-apple-pear relish, 120–25
Cranberry salad, 24–29
Cream, strawberry Devonshire, 63

D

Desserts
  Bartlett pear squares, 19
  gingerbread cookies, 130–33
  Kahlúa strawberry charlotte, 50–51
  peach-raspberry chocolate tart, 94
  plum tart, 114
  pumpkin gingerbread, 116–19
  rhubarb cobbler, 55
  rose geranium sorbet, 96–101
  rum-spiked rice pudding, 20–23
  sugar cookies, 128
  sugar on snow, 42
  See also Cakes; Ice cream; Pies
Dilled Green Bean Salad, 101
Dilled havarti, 96–101
Dill pickle salad, 130–33

E

Easy Sugar Cookies, 128
Eggs
  herbed scrambled, 60–63
  soft-cooked, 134–37
Espresso, 48–51

F

Fiddlehead ferns, 52–55
Finnish yellow potatoes, 30–35
French fries, 84–87
Fresh Peach-Raspberry Chocolate Tart, 94

Fried chicken, 64–67, 91
Fruits
    autumn seasonal, 134–37
    basket, 64–67
    pies, 88–91
    See also specific fruits
Fudge, maple, 40–43
Funnel cakes, 84–87

G

Garden greens, 88–91
Garden salad, 92–95
Garden vegetables, 92–95
Gingerbread, pumpkin, 116–19
Gingerbread cookies, 130–33
Goose, roast, 29
Grape juice, 130–33
Grapes, 130–33
Green beans, 120–25
    salad, dilled, 101
Green pea and potato bisque, 130–33
Green salad, 36–39, 96–101, 112–15
Grilled vegetables, 112–15
Guacamole, 102–7

H

Ham, 56–59
    and cheese and onion pie, 132
Hearth bread, 116–19
Herbed cheese dip, 92–95
Herbed pork lion, 40–43
Herbed scrambled eggs, 60–63
Herb tea, 24–29
Honey Berry Butter, 63
Honeydew with lemon verbena,
    96–101
Hot buttered biscuits, 20–23
Hot buttered rum, 20–23
Hot chocolate, 20–23

I

Ice cream, 88–91
    butter pecan, 102–7
    chocolate, with Cointreau, 36–39
    maple, 40–43
    mince or apple pie with, 24–29
    praline, 116–19
    vanilla, 60–63, 120–25

J

Jarlsberg, Ham, and Onion Pie,
    132

K

Kahlúa Strawberry Charlotte,
    50–51

L

Lamb, roast rack of, 112–15
Leaf lettuce salad, 52–55
Lemonade, 84–87
Lemon tarts, 126–29
Lettuce with herbs, 64–67

M

Maple baked beans, 40–43
Maple butter, bread with, 40–43
Maple fudge, 40–43
Maple ice cream, 40–43
Maple sugar, on snow, 42
Maple sugar pie, 40–43
Marinated vegetable salad, 30–35
Meats
    sliced, 134–37
    See also specific meats
Milk, 134–37
Mince pie with cinnamon ice cream,
    24–29
Mint Julep, 59
Muesli, 137
Muffins, corn, 56–59

Muscadine sauce, 24–29
Mushrooms
    and beef stew, 22
    chicken pie with, 36–39

N

Nuts, spiced, 116–19

O

Oatmeal Bread, 73
Onions, and cheese and ham pie, 132
Onions, potatoes, corn on the cob,
    78–83
Orange juice, 134–37
Oysters, roasted, 36–39

P

Pancakes, 60–63
    apple, 30–35
Parker house rolls, 24–29
Peach anticipation, 48–51
Pears, 130–33
    squares, 19
Pecan pie, 120–25
Pepper and dried tomato brioche,
    112–15
Pernod, 96–101
Pies
    apple, 102–7
    chicken and mushroom, 36–39
    fruit, 88–91
    Jarlsberg, ham, and onion, 132
    maple sugar, 40–43
    mince or apple, 24–29
    pecan, 120–25
    pumpkin, 120–25
    ramp and asparagus, 52–55
Plum tart, 114
Popcorn, 30–35
Pork loin, 40–43
Pork shiitake pâté, 64–67

Potatoes
    baby red, 52–55
    Finnish yellow, 30–35
    French fried, 84–87
    salad, 102–7
Poultry. *See* Chicken; Goose; Turkey
Preserves, 134–37
Prizewinning Cocoa Cake, 87
Pudding, rum-spiked rice, 20–23
Pumpernickel bread, 30–35
Pumpkin, beef and vegetable stew
    in, 116–19
Pumpkin Gingerbread, 116–19
Pumpkin pie, 120–25
Pumpkin seeds, 116–19

R

Raclette, 35
Raisins, 134–37
Ramp and asparagus pie, 52–55
Raspberries
    champagne and, 36–39
    coconut cake with, 56–59
    ginger punch, 126–29
Ratatouille, 64–67
Red and green cabbage slaw, 40–43
Red potatoes, 52–55
Rhubarb Cobbler, 55
Rice pudding, 20–23
Roasted oysters, 36–39
Roast Goose, 29
Roast Turkey, 125
Rolls
    cloverleaf, 48–51
    Parker house, 24–29
Rose geranium sorbet, 96–101
Rum, hot buttered, 20–23
Rum-spiked rice pudding, 20–23

S

Sage bread, 96–101
Salads
    avocado, 16–19
    Boston bibb, 116–19
    cabbage slaw, 40–43
    cole slaw, 107

cranberry, 24–29
dilled green bean, 101
dill pickle, 130–33
garden, 92–95
green, 36–39, 96–101, 112–15
leaf lettuce, 52–55
lettuce with herbs, 64–67
potato, 102–7
rice, turkey breast with, 48–51
tossed green, 56–59
vegetable, 30–35, 88–91
Salmon steaks, 92–95
Sauces
honey berry butter, 63
maple butter, 40–43
maple fudge, 40–43
muscadine, 24–29
strawberry Devonshire cream, 63
Sausage and pepper sandwiches,
84–87
Sausages, 30–35
Scones, 126–29
Seafood
chowder, 24–29
roasted oysters, 36–39
salmon steaks, 92–95
steamed lobster, chicken, and
clams, 78–83
Sesame seeds, 134–37
Shortbread hearts, 36–39

Soups
chestnut, 120–25
clam chowder, 78–83
green pea and potato bisque,
130–33
seafood chowder, 24–29
Sour cream, 60–63
Sourdough bread, 64–67
Spiced tea, 126–29
Spritzer, 64–67
Steamed lobster, chicken, and clams,
78–83
Stews
baked beef and mushroom, 22
beef and chicken, 16–19
beef and vegetable, 116–19
Strawberries
honey berry butter, 63
preserves, 60–63
shortcake, 60–63
Strawberry charlotte, 50–51
Strawberry Devonshire Cream,
63
Stuffing, chestnut, 24–29
Succotash, 24–29
Sugar, 60–63
Sugar cookies, 128
Sugar on Snow, 42
Sunflower seeds, 134–37
Sweet potatoes, 120–25
with apples, 24–29

T
Tarts
lemon, 126–29
peach-raspberry chocolate, 94
plum, 114
Tea sandwiches, 126–29
Texas toast, 102–7
Tossed green salad, 56–59
Turkey
breast, and rice salad on spring
greens, 48–51
cooking method, 125
with oyster stuffing, 120–25
and rice salad, 48–51

V
Valentine Biscuits, 39
Vanilla ice cream, 60–63
Vegetables
autumn greens, 120–25
garden, 92–95
garden greens, 88–91
grilled, 112–15
salad, 30–35, 88–91
See also specific vegetables

W
Waffles, 60–63
Warm rum-spiked rice pudding,
20–23
Watermelon, 78–83
Whipped cream, 60–63
Wine, 92–95, 96–101
German wine labels, 73

Y
Yogurt, 60–63

Z
Zucchini, 92–95
bread, 92–95

ADDITIONAL PHOTO CREDITS

Pages 2–3 © D. Radcliffe/FPG International,
Pages 8–9 (l to r) © Burke/Triolo, © Dennis M. Gottlieb, © Burke/Triolo,
Pages 14–15 © Christopher C. Bain, Page 30 Courtesy Wisconsin Milk Marketing Board,
Page 32 © Christopher C. Bain, Pages 46–47 © Sam Saylor, Page 48 © W. Atlee Burpee & Co.,
Page 50 © Burke/Triolo, Page 52 © Steven Mark Needham/Envision,
Page 63 © Dennis M. Gottlieb, Pages 76–77 © Sam Saylor, Page 85 © Steven Mark
Needham/Envision, Page 104 © Steven Mark Needham/Envision, Pages 110–111 © Sam Saylor,
Page 112 © Dennis M. Gottlieb, Page 123 © Burke/Triolo,
Page 130 © Dennis M. Gottlieb